CITIZENSHIP

Citizenship has become one of the most important political ideas of our time. It is an idea that at once recognises the individual's entitlement to rights and the collective responsibilities on which stable governance rests. In this clear and comprehensive overview of the subject Keith Faulks explores citizenship's historical and conceptual origins, its contemporary dilemmas and its emancipatory potential for the future. Among the questions the author addresses are:

- Can citizenship exist without the nation-state?
- What should the balance be between our rights and responsibilities?
- Should we enjoy group as well as individual rights?
- Is citizenship relevant to our private as well as our public lives?
- Have processes of globalisation rendered citizenship redundant?

Keith Faulks is Subject Leader in Politics at the University of Central Lancashire.

KEY IDEAS

SERIES EDITOR: PETER HAMILTON, THE OPEN UNIVERSITY, MILTON KEYNES

Designed to complement the successful *Key Sociologists*, this series covers the main concepts, issues, debates, and controversies in sociology and the social sciences. The series aims to provide authoritative essays on central topics of social science, such as community, power, work, sexuality, inequality, benefits and ideology, class, family, etc. Books adopt a strong individual 'line' constituting original essays rather than literary surveys, and form lively and original treatments of their subject matter. The books will be useful to students and teachers of sociology, political science, economics, psychology, philosophy, and geography.

Anti-racism
ALASTAIR BONNETT

Class
STEPHEN EDGELL

Consumption
ROBERT BOCOCK

Culture
CHRIS JENKS

Globalization
MALCOLM WATERS

Lifestyle
DAVID CHANEY

Mass Media
PIERRE SORLIN

Moral Panics
KENNETH THOMPSON

Postmodernity
BARRY SMART

Racism
ROBERT MILES

Risk
DEBORAH LUPTON

Sexuality
JEFFREY WEEKS

The Symbolic Construction of Community
ANTHONY P. COHEN

CITIZENSHIP

Keith Faulks

Routledge
Taylor & Francis Group

LONDON AND NEW YORK

First published 2000
by Routledge
2 Park Square, Milton Park, Abingdon, Oxon OX14 4RN

Simultaneously published in the USA and Canada
by Routledge
270 Madison Ave, New York, NY 10016

Transferred to Digital Printing 2003

Routledge is an imprint of the Taylor & Francis Group, an informa business

British Library Cataloguing in Publication Data
A catalogue record for this book is available from the British Library

Library of Congress Cataloging in Publication Data
Faulks, Keith.
    Citizenship / Keith Faulks.
        p.   cm. – (Key ideas)
    Includes bibliographical references and index.
        1. Citizenship.   I. Title.   II. Series.

JF801 .F38 2000
323.6–dc21   00–029107

ISBN 10: 0-415-19633-7 (hbk)
ISBN 10: 0-415-19634-5 (pbk)

ISBN 13: 978-0-415-19633-8 (hbk)
ISBN 13: 978-0-415-19634-5 (pbk)

For my parents
Robin and Patricia Faulks

Contents

PREFACE

On the day that I started writing this book, the British government announced that it was introducing compulsory citizenship
education into schools. Listening to a television debate on the
merits and pitfalls of this policy that evening, I felt somewhat
encouraged in the task that lay ahead. Citizenship has become a
buzzword, but like so many ideas that share that dubious honour,
it is often misunderstood. Despite the fact that the panellists
included prominent politicians, I was struck by how confused
their understanding of citizenship was. It seems, then, a good
time to write a book on the subject – as well as to start teaching
it to our children!

In this work, I present a theoretical overview of some current
debates and controversies surrounding the concept of citizenship.
In keeping with the spirit of the *Key Ideas* series, however, I try
to avoid drowning the reader in a 'sea of summaries'. The relevant
literature is now vast; partly a legacy of citizenship's buzzword
status, and partly reflecting citizenship's importance as an idea
that has relevance to today's social and political problems. It

would therefore be an impossible task to review all of these often insightful contributions. Instead, I adopt a particular line of argument in each chapter and offer my own perspectives on citizenship. My approach is largely conceptual, rather than historical or comparative, and the examples I use to illustrate the discussion are drawn from those societies I know best. However, it will become obvious, particularly to those who make it as far as chapter 6, that I consider citizenship crucial to solving global as well as local problems. Chapter 1 provides an overview of the concept and outlines the book's structure and arguments – readers are therefore advised to begin there.

While writing this book, I have been lucky enough to receive support from a number of friends and colleagues. Particular thanks are due to Stevie Hallows, John Hoffman, Joe Ravetz, Alex Thomson and Robert Gibb who during the last few years have willingly listened to and criticised my thoughts on citizenship. I am also grateful to Susan Gray who collected mountains of material for me to read for this project and who served as a very able proofreader. Finally, I would like to express my gratitude to all at Routledge and especially to Mari Shullaw who has been very supportive.

I dedicate this book to my parents, with thanks for all they have done for me over the years.

1

THE IDEA OF CITIZENSHIP

Citizenship has an almost universal appeal. Radicals and conservatives alike feel able to utilise the language of citizenship in
support of their policy prescriptions. This is because citizenship
contains both individualistic and collectivist elements. Liberals
value citizenship because the rights it bestows give space to
the individual to pursue their interests free from interference.
Rights, in their political form, also enable the individual to have
a hand in shaping common governmental institutions. Citizenship therefore also has great appeal as an inherently relational
idea that entails cooperation between individuals in the running
of their lives. Indeed, the concept of the 'private citizen' is an
oxymoron (Oldfield 1990: 159). This means that in addition to
rights, citizenship entails duties and obligations. Even a state
like the USA, which is often said to place too little significance
upon responsibilities, has an oath of allegiance that includes such
duties as supporting the constitution, undertaking military
service, and even to 'perform work of national importance when
required by law'. All political communities, of whatever political

persuasion, must make demands upon their citizens. Citizenship therefore appeals to conservatives, communitarians and ecologists, all of whom stress the responsibilities we all have to sustain our political communities and the natural environment. For only in this communal context are sustainable human relationships, and therefore rights, feasible.

Since the late 1980s, thinkers on the left have also embraced citizenship as a potentially radical ideal. There have always been socialists who have seen the democratic potential of citizenship. However, in the past, the general attitude of those on the left was one of suspicion. Citizenship was seen as part of the problem rather than a solution to the injustices of capitalism. Indeed, the rights of citizenship seemed to be imbued with a capitalist logic. They helped legitimise private property and hid the inequalities of class society behind an abstract rhetoric of equality. The failure of communism, the decline of class organisation, and the realisation that in increasingly heterogeneous societies not all inequalities can be reduced to questions of economics, have led many socialists to reconsider their rejection of citizenship. Feminists, too, have found citizenship useful in conceptualising the roots of women's oppression. Feminist analysis of the gendered nature of citizenship has helped draw our attention away from questions concerned purely with rights and duties, towards the question of the nature of the community in which citizenship is exercised. Poverty, discrimination and exclusion can all undermine the benefits of citizenship. Thus, a consideration of citizenship must also involve an examination of the conditions that make it meaningful.

While there is a consensus that citizenship is a desirable thing, there is much less agreement about what the status should entail, what kind of community best promotes citizenship, and whether the status is inherently exclusive. This book explores such questions and suggests answers to some of them. I will be concerned primarily with the nature and limits of liberal citizenship. This is because it is through a debate with liberalism that the majority of contemporary accounts of citizenship have developed. Consequently, from this point on, I will desist from adding the term liberal or modern when discussing citizenship, unless drawing comparison with an earlier form of the idea. In this opening chapter, I provide a conceptual and historical overview. This will set the scene for the analysis of the dilemmas of liberal citizenship contained in chapters 2 to 7.

A CONCEPTUAL OVERVIEW

Modern citizenship is inherently egalitarian. This has not always been the case. It is only with the development of liberal tradition, which I take to be synonymous with modernity, that citizenship has developed such universality. In its liberal form, citizenship has lent great weight to arguments by minorities who can point to unequal treatment as an infringement of their basic rights, upon which their human dignity rests. Campaigns for the extension of citizenship have ranged from the anti-slavery movement in Britain in the eighteenth century, women's movements demanding the vote in the early twentieth century, African Americans in the 1960s campaigning for basic civil rights, to gay activists in the 1990s protesting that the age of consent be equalised with heterosexuals. Such campaigns have all drawn upon citizenship's capacity to act as what John Hoffman (1997) calls a 'momentum concept'. Citizenship contains an internal logic that demands that its benefits necessarily become ever more universal and egalitarian. Since citizenship gained currency in modern politics, its force has proved difficult for elites to resist. For this reason, Turner (1986: xii, 135) has contended that the modern history of citizenship,

> can be conceived as a series of expanding circles which are
> pushed forward by the momentum of conflict and struggle

> ... The movement of citizenship is from the particular to the universal, since particular definitions of persons for the purpose of exclusion appear increasingly irrational and incongruent with the basis of the modern polity.

Unlike slaves, vassals or subjects, whose statuses imply hierarchy and domination, citizens formally enjoy legitimate and equal membership of a society. If it is to have substance, therefore, citizenship cannot allow arbitrary treatment: citizens must be judged by objective and transparent criteria. Citizenship also acknowledges individuals' ability to make judgements about their own lives, which is not predetermined by their 'race', religion, class, gender or any other single part of their identity. As such, citizenship, more than any other identity, is able to satisfy the basic political impulse of humans, which Hegel has termed the need for recognition (see Williams 1997: 59–64). The status of citizen implies a sense of inclusion into the wider community. It recognises the contribution a particular individual makes to that community, while at the same time granting him or her individual autonomy. This autonomy is reflected in a set of rights which, though varying in content enormously over time and space, always imply recognition of political agency on the part of the bearer of those rights. Thus, a key defining characteristic of citizenship, and what differentiates it most from mere subjecthood, is an ethic of participation. Citizenship is an active rather than passive status. In short, citizenship is incompatible with domination, whether the source of that domination be the state, the family, the husband, the church, the ethnic group, or any other force that seeks to deny us recognition as an autonomous individual, capable of self-governance.

The appeal of citizenship, however, is not just the benefits it gives to the individual. Citizenship is always a reciprocal and, therefore, social idea. It can never be purely a set of rights that free the individual from obligations to others. Rights always require a framework for their recognition and mechanisms through which they can be fulfilled. Such a social framework, which includes courts, schools, hospitals and parliaments, requires that citizens all play their part to maintain it. This means that citizenship implies duties and obligations, as well as rights. Indeed, it is conceivable that society could function justly without a formal expression of rights. It is, however, difficult to imagine a stable human community without some sense of obligation between its members. Citizenship is therefore an excellent basis for human governance.

Governance refers to the inherent human need to create and maintain social order and to distribute material and cultural resources. Politics, to which citizenship is closely related, is a set of methods and techniques, such as deliberation, compromise, diplomacy, and power sharing, through which the problem of governance can be resolved non-violently. The use of violence in human relationships, whether these relationships take place in the private or public sphere, represents the failure of politics rather than an intrinsic element of political life. Politics is concerned therefore with achieving and sustaining consensual governance. Citizenship is pivotal to the achievement of this goal precisely because it provides a strong legitimising identity. By demanding that we treat individuals equally, citizenship can negate sources of social tension that may threaten social order. Through its package of rights, duties and obligations, citizenship provides a way of distributing and managing resources justly, by sharing the benefits and burdens of social life.

Citizenship then is a powerful idea. It recognises the dignity of the individual but at the same time reaffirms the social context in which the individual acts. Citizenship is therefore an excellent example of what Anthony Giddens (1984: 25) has called the 'duality of structure'. For Giddens, the individual and the community cannot accurately be understood as opposed and antagonistic ideas. Instead, individual agency and social practices are mutually dependent. Through exercising rights and obligations, individuals reproduce the necessary conditions for citizenship.

Citizenship is therefore a dynamic identity. As creative agents, citizens will always find new ways to express their citizenship, and new rights, duties and institutions will need to be constructed to give form to the changing needs and aspirations of the citizen and community. As citizenship is about human relationships, it defies a simple, static definition that can be applied to all societies at all times. Instead, the idea of citizenship is inherently contested and contingent, always reflecting the particular set of relationships and types of governance found within any given society. This means that one of the essential questions we must ask when trying to understand citizenship is what social and political arrangements form the context in which it is practised. Indeed, one of my major criticisms of much of the existing literature on citizenship is that it fails to pay enough attention to this question of context.

Many thinkers from the liberal tradition have advanced normative theories explaining what the citizen can expect in the way of rights and duties, without considering in enough depth the constraints that class, gender and ethnic differences (amongst many other social divisions) place upon individual citizens. Since all citizenship rights involve the distribution of resources, and because obligations are exercised within a societal context, any discussion of citizenship is also a consideration of power. If society fails to provide the necessary resources to sustain rights, as socialists have often feared, rights become a sham. Similarly, if the institutions in which obligations are exercised are designed to favour one group over another then again citizenship is diminished. In their obsession with defending abstract individual rights, liberals have often overlooked the power structures that can either facilitate or constrain citizens in the exercise of their rights and in the performance of their responsibilities.

Citizenship is portrayed by liberals as part of an evolutionary process towards a more rational, just and well-governed society (Marshall 1992). This ignores why citizenship changes over time and the interests that are served by such shifts in its meaning. In practice, citizenship can be diluted as well as enhanced. The processes that determine how citizenship is defined are bound up with questions of self-interest, power and conflict. For example, citizens' rights are intimately linked to the priorities and irrationalities of the market and the states system. Economic crises may well lead to a reduction in rights, as social entitlements are rolled back in the name of industrial competitiveness. Warfare between states, or internal social conflict within a state, may also radically change the meaning of citizenship: participants in warfare being rewarded with more extensive rights, for example, or a particular social movement effectively mobilising in such a way as to promote an extension of its members' entitlements.

This brings us to three further questions, in addition to that of context, that we must address in exploring the idea of citizenship. First, social struggles have often been concerned with the *extent* of citizenship: who should be regarded as a citizen and what criteria, if any, are legitimate in excluding some from the benefits of citizenship? Second, what should the *content* of citizenship be in terms of rights, duties and obligations? Third, how *deep* or *thick* should our conception of citizenship be? By this, I mean how demanding or extensive should our identity as citizens be and to what extent should it take precedence over other sources of social identity and competing claims we have upon our time, such as family commitments or making a living?

Regarding the extent of citizenship, to ask who is to be included as a citizen is also to ask who is to be excluded from the status. All states, however liberal their immigration laws, impose controls upon who can become resident within their territory, and under what conditions they can remain. Thus, citizenship is closely associated with nationality, with the two terms often being used interchangeably in international law. Historically, the extent of citizenship has consequently always been limited. For the individual then, and in particular the refugee or immigrant, the primary question of citizenship is often that of social membership. In the contemporary world, this means membership of a state. To be deprived of citizenship of a state, when the state is the key distributor of social resources, is to be deprived of the basis of other rights. This is why the United Nations Universal Declaration of Human Rights (Article 15.1) includes the right to citizenship as a fundamental human right upon which the protection of other entitlements is premised.

Because of its importance to the idea of citizenship, chapter 2 is devoted to an exploration of the nation-state. It is no coincidence that the idea of citizenship has become more prominent in political discourse whenever the nature of political community has been transformed. The formation of the polis in ancient Greece or the expansion of the Roman Empire, for example, both required a rethinking of the meaning of citizenship amongst politicians and theorists alike. In terms of modern citizenship, the key event was the French Revolution, which fused citizenship with the nation-state. Chapter 2 first discusses the implications of this fusion. I will then address the question of whether citizenship requires nationality to give it meaning. Finally, some examples of current debates in Europe will be used to illustrate some of the controversies and contradictions of a citizenship that is defined as membership of the nation-state. I will argue that in order to unlock the inclusive potential of citizenship, the concept must be freed from its association with the nation-state.

The extent of citizenship is a question as much about groups within the state, who may be formally or informally excluded from citizenship, as it is about questions of immigration and asylum. The campaigns to extend citizenship mentioned above are good examples of how marginalised groups *within* the state have had to apply pressure to privileged elites in order to remove unjustifiable restrictions upon the practice of citizenship. Thus, the extent and content of citizenship is intimately bound up with the context of this status. It may be that women, for instance, are formally viewed as equal citizens with men. If, however, women exercise their citizenship within the constraints of a patriarchal system, in substantive terms their citizenship is worth less than that of men.

I analyse some of the controversies surrounding the appropriate content of citizenship in chapter 3. In particular, the apparent tensions between different kinds of rights and between rights and responsibilities are analysed. The contemporary debate concerning these issues has taken the form of a dialogue between the dominant liberal approach and critical perspectives such as Marxism, communitarianism and feminism. My argument will draw upon these critiques. I will contend that liberalism, largely because of its assumptions about the state and the market, embraces an abstract and thin conception of citizenship. However, we cannot simply reverse liberalism's emphasis upon rights and assert in its place an ethic of responsibility as many conservatives and communitarians have advocated. Instead, for citizenship to have meaning we must see rights and responsibilities as mutually supportive.

Chapter 4 tackles the problem of difference. I ask whether the universal citizenship associated with liberalism is compatible with the pluralist reality of modern society. Should the content of citizenship vary from group to group and should minorities be protected from the majority through the provision of special rights? In critically assessing the answers to this question provided by such pluralists as Young (1990) and Kymlicka (1995), my conclusion is that so-called group rights create more problems than they solve. The point is not to give up on liberal citizenship; it is to fulfil the promise of liberal citizenship by transforming the context in which it is practised. The key to rendering citizenship more inclusive is to recognise the inherently racialised, patriarchal and class-based nature of the state and the corrosive effects of the free market upon rights and responsibilities.

The final dimension of citizenship I shall discuss is that of 'depth' or 'thickness'. Clarke (1996: 4) defines 'deep' citizenship as

> the activity of the citizen self acting in a variety of places and spaces. That activity shifts the centre of politics away from the state and so recovers the possibility of politics as an individual participation in a shared and communal activity.

Tilly (1995: 8) contrasts thin and thick conceptions of citizenship as follows: citizenship can be

> thin where it entails few transactions, rights and obligations; thick where it occupies a significant share of all transactions, rights and obligations sustained by state agents and people living under their jurisdiction.

Tilly's definition is more conventional in its identification of citizenship with the state, while Clarke argues that citizenship must extend beyond state borders. Both however raise such questions as: is citizenship purely of public significance, or can it pervade private lives as well? What is the significance of citizenship relative to other demands upon our time and enthusiasm? Bubeck (1995) has provided a useful typology that contrasts thick conceptions of citizenship with thin or procedural notions, which I have adapted in Table 1.1.

I believe, along with other critics of liberalism, that the citizenship liberals advocate has been too thin and has been subordinate to market principles and the interests of political and economic elites. Chapter 5 explores how the emancipatory potential of citizenship can be fulfilled through policies aimed at transforming the balance between rights and responsibilities and between the market and democracy.

Table 1.1 Ideal types of thin and thick conceptions of citizenship

Thin citizenship	Thick citizenship
Rights privileged	Rights and responsibilities as mutually supportive
Passive	Active
State as a necessary evil	Political community (not necessarily the state) as the foundation of the good life
Purely public status	Pervades public and private
Independence	Interdependence
Freedom through choice	Freedom through civic virtue
Legal	Moral

In chapter 6, I explore how globalisation is transforming the context of citizenship and therefore requires that we rethink citizenship's content, extent and depth. Could it be that contemporary social change has rendered citizenship outmoded? Certainly some theories of postnational citizenship imply that citizenship will be increasingly replaced by the more inclusive idea of human rights that extend to all people regardless of their nationality (Soysal 1994). Globalisation has also impacted upon the debate over content and depth. Ecologists, for instance, have pointed to the need to balance human rights with greater obligations to nature and to future generations. I agree that in order to fulfil its universalistic potential citizenship must look beyond the state. This should, as ecologists suggest, involve international obligations as well as human rights. However, citizenship also requires a political community to have meaning. I therefore consider the extent to which developments such as the European Union are providing a new context for what Heater (1990: 314) refers to as multiple citizenship.

In chapters 2 to 6, I implicitly develop what I shall call a postmodern theory of citizenship. The main elements of this theory are summarised in chapter 7, which brings the book's arguments together in the form of a conclusion. Very briefly, this perspective attempts to combine the insights of several traditions of citizenship theory to construct a rich and rounded theory of citizenship, which I would describe as post-, rather than anti-, liberal. Thus, my theory departs from many exponents of postmodernism who offer powerful critiques of modernist ideologies, but then fail to develop alternative conceptual tools that can be used to reconstruct the nature of governance.

The socialist critique of liberal citizenship retains much of its power in that it highlights the relative neglect of issues of power inequality by liberals, which in practice negate the positive effects of citizenship. Ironically, however, many socialists commit the same error as liberals in their emphasis upon the economic at the expense of the political. Too often socialism has failed to appreciate the need for citizenship as a necessary element of governance, preferring instead to pin its hopes on revolution or upon social engineering by the state: strategies which both undermine the attributes of good citizenship (Selbourne 1994). Republicanism, by itself, cannot generate a convincing theory of citizenship because it shares with liberalism a rather abstract approach to politics. It has the virtue, however, of placing citizenship at the heart of its philosophy, where politics, not economics, is seen as primary. Republicanism is also more willing than liberalism to demand duties and obligations from the citizen (Pettit 1997). It will become apparent that the insights of ecological and feminist thought are also important to my theory of citizenship. As the risk of global ecological disaster intensifies, citizenship must be sensitive to the needs of the environment, and indeed these are indivisible from the needs of citizens. Feminism shares with socialism a desire for human emancipation that recognises and removes the discriminatory barriers, of whatever kind, to the exercise of citizenship. The ethic of care advanced by some feminists has a part to play in a reformulated theory of citizenship. Care implies the recognition of the social nature and interdependence of all citizens and helps challenge the abstract liberal notion of independent citizens.

I would stress, however, that my theory seeks to build upon the strengths of liberalism, which are considerable. These strengths will become clear in the course of this volume. Unlike conservatism or some forms of republicanism, liberalism is at heart a perfectionist theory, which stresses our ability as humans to create and improve our systems of governance. It seems to me that such a view of human nature is the only one compatible with democratic citizenship. To assert that 'natural inequalities' are insurmountable barriers to people's ability, in cooperation with others, to shape their destinies through the exercise of citizenship, is to allow theoretical space for advocates of subjecthood, domination, elite rule, or some other such hierarchical system of governance.

To summarise the discussion so far: citizenship is a membership status, which contains a package of rights, duties and obligations, and which implies equality, justice and autonomy. Its development and nature at any given time can be understood through a consideration of the interconnected dimensions of context, extent, content and depth. A rich sense of citizenship can only be achieved when the contextual barriers to its performance are recognised and removed. The theory of postmodern citizenship, developed in this book, provides a perspective on how this might be achieved. In the rest of this chapter, a historical overview will provide necessary background for our understanding of the context in which the controversies of modern citizenship have emerged.

A HISTORICAL OVERVIEW

The idea of citizenship, like so many important concepts of social science, has its origins in ancient Greece. The work of Aristotle (1992) represents the first systematic attempt to develop a theory of citizenship, while the practice of citizenship found its first institutional expression in the Greek polis, notably in Athens from the fifth century until the fourth century BC. The citizenship of the Greeks, however, was very different in its form and function from citizenship in the modern period. It is therefore common among historians of citizenship to divide the development of citizenship into distinct stages, to highlight the shifting meaning of the concept, from its origins in the ancient world to modernity and beyond (Heater 1990; Riesenberg 1992). Riesenberg, for example, identifies the first stage of citizenship as beginning with the Greeks and ending with the onset of modernity, marked above all by the French Revolution of 1789. Riesenberg's two-stage approach is too general and conflates the diverse ideas of citizenship that existed in ancient Greece, Rome and the medieval city. The instrumentalism of Machiavelli's republican citizenship for instance, which was aimed primarily at securing order in medieval Florence, was very different from citizenship as the political expression of human nature that can be found in Aristotle. Held (1996: 36–69) makes a useful distinction in this regard between the protective republicanism of Machiavelli and the developmental republicanism associated with Aristotle. Machiavelli viewed citizenship as a method for asserting citizens' interests, whereas Aristotle felt the performance of citizenship was of far more profound significance, as a core element of what it means to be human. Such diversity should caution us against talking of a single pre-modern conception of citizenship. It is also a mistake to assume that modernist understandings of citizenship were created in a vacuum. In reality, modern citizenship has built upon ancient and pre-modern ideas and therefore continuities as well as contrasts can be found in the history of citizenship. The values of universality and equality, so important to modern citizenship, had their theoretical roots partly in the works of the Greek Stoic philosophers, who asserted the moral equality of human beings. In addition, the liberal discourse of natural rights drew inspiration from the universalistic tradition of Roman natural law.

It is perhaps more fruitful to draw contrasts between modern citizenship and its historical predecessors in terms of the four dimensions of citizenship outlined above. When discussed in terms of context, extent, content and depth, clear differences do emerge between the citizenship of modernity and its historical predecessors. These contrasts are discussed below, and a comparison is drawn in Table 1.2 between citizenship in the modern state, and its polar opposite, the ancient Athenian polis.

Recent scholarship confirms the dangers of imposing modernist assumptions when analysing the nature of citizenship in ancient Greece. Manville (1994), in advancing what he terms the new

Table 1.2 Citizenship in the ancient Greek polis and the modern state

	Polis	*Modern state*
Type of community	Organic	Legal/Differentiated association
Scale	Small	Large
Depth of citizenship	Thick	Thin
Extent of citizenship	Exclusive and inequality naturalised	Progressively inclusive and theoretically egalitarian, but limited by statist context
Content of citizenship	Extensive obligations	Rights and limited duties
Context of citizenship	Slave society, agricultural production	Patriarchal, racialised and capitalist states system, industrial production

paradigm of Athenian citizenship, argues that the dualisms that shape modern politics, such as a divide between state and society, between public and private, or between law and morality, simply did not apply in Athens. Instead, the context of Greek citizenship was that of the small-scale, organic community of the polis. Citizens ran their own affairs, acting as both legislators and executors, and defended themselves through a highly developed sense of military obligation. Such was the importance of warfare to citizenship that Weber (1958: 220) refers to the polis as a 'warriors' guild'. Other scholars have noted how the changing nature of military tactics in the polis influenced the practice of citizenship. Riesenberg (1992: 9) highlights the importance of the military formation known as the phalanx from the eighth century BC onwards. This tactic relied upon close cooperation between each soldier and, Riesenberg argues, was an important step towards a relational conception of citizenship, for men at least. Thus in Greece, a connection between war, citizenship and masculinity was established that would reappear repeatedly in the subsequent history of citizenship.

Owing to the organic nature of the polis, there was no sense in which citizenship could be seen as a purely public matter, divorced from the private life of the individual. The obligations of citizenship permeated all aspects of life in the polis: 'citizenship and the polis [were] one and the same' (Manville 1994: 24). A civic ideology dominated politics and society in ancient Greece. This ideology underpinned all educational, leisure and governmental institutions, each of which was concerned with the exercise and promotion of active citizenship: 'every civic institution taught a pattern of values that was viewed as ancient, immutable, and of divine origin' (Riesenberg 1992: 35). This meant that from birth, citizens internalised the values of active citizenship, greatly influencing the content and depth of its practice.

The polis was considered as prior to, and constitutive of, the individual. Aristotle (1992) famously expressed this idea in his argument that to take no part in the running of the community's affairs is to be either a beast or a God! To be truly human one had to be a citizen, and an active citizen at that (Clarke 1994: 3–7). Thus citizenship was obligations-based rather than rights-based, since the close identification individuals felt between their own destinies and that of their community rendered the notion of asserting one's rights against the interests of the wider community inconceivable. Obligations generally did not take the form of statutory duties. They were perceived by citizens as opportunities to be virtuous and to serve the community. The institutions of government provided many opportunities for the exercise of this civic virtue and were modelled on the maxim that all citizens should be both ruler and ruled. In Athens, in particular, important political and judicial offices were rotated through a system of lot and all citizens had the right to speak and vote in the political assembly. It is true that in 594/3 BC, when Solon reclassified the various categories of Athenian citizens in response to growing social unrest and demands for inclusion by previously excluded classes, some groups were still afforded more political influence than others. Manville (1994) makes the point, however, that citizenship was not, as is commonly argued, determined by wealth. Instead, the level of participation afforded to each group was ultimately for the community to decide politically.

Moreover, following the revision of the Athenian constitution in 400 BC, the importance of political participation was recognised through publicly funded payments for citizens who attended the assembly. Crucially then, despite resistance from some elites within the polis, the Athenians recognised the importance of the material foundation of citizenship. Poverty was seen as a barrier to citizenship and thus payments for the exercise of citizenship can be seen as an important symbol of the dominance of politics over economics in the collective priorities of the polis.

Citizenship had then a holistic nature that is perhaps hard to appreciate in our own time, where politics is viewed with suspicion, and obligation is seen as at best a necessary evil, at worst an infringement of our freedom. To the citizen of the polis, civic virtue *was* freedom, and the primary source of honour and respect. Because civic virtue was so central to the individual's sense of self-worth and purpose, citizenship was both deep and thick in the sense that 'life and identity were offered and defined by the polis almost exclusively: even the family was hardly competitive in the totality of its demands and gifts' (Riesenberg 1992: 25). Even the Greeks' concepts of morality and the good were very different from our own. As Jordan (1989: 67) argues, 'there was no clash between citizenship obligations and the duties of private morality because there was no such thing as private morality'. Similarly, the idea of the 'good' was not understood as being expressed via a private code of ethics. Instead, the good was to be found through service to the community in the form of military obligation and political participation. In short, morality and the good life were both expressed publicly through the performance of civic virtue.

The status of citizenship in the polis was, however, highly exclusive. In fact, the primary difference between pre-modern and modern citizenship is that in ancient Greece and Rome, as well as in those cities that practised citizenship in the middle ages, inequality of status was accepted without question. Indeed, citizenship was valued in part because of its exclusive nature and as a mark of superiority over non-citizens, whether they be women, slaves or 'barbarians'. The Greeks, for instance, saw the institutions of slavery and empire as entirely compatible with citizenship. Some scholars have asserted that an extensive citizenship for the privileged, and particularly the benefits paid to citizens through taxation, were made possible by the community's dependence upon these unjust institutions. This interpretation is simplistic, however. In fact, the democratic elements of citizenship, as well as payment for participation in civic affairs, continued well after the loss of the Athenian Empire (Arblaster 1994: 23). It is nonetheless true to say that hierarchy and exclusion were seen as axiomatic in ancient Greece. Slaves were not the only ones excluded from citizenship. Women were seen as lacking the necessary rationality required for political participation. Additionally, at certain times, the Athenian polis applied strict criteria to the question of which residents qualified for citizenship status. In 451–450 BC, under the leadership of Pericles, citizenship was restricted to only those residents whose parents were both born in the polis.

Roman conceptions of citizenship, in contrast to Greek exclusivity, became increasingly inclusive in their reach as its empire expanded. At the time of the republic, citizenship, as in Greece, was a privileged status, tied closely to political participation. However, in Rome's imperial age, citizenship gradually lost its association with participation and instead became a tool of social control and pacification. The Romans found that by granting citizenship to the peoples of the empire, something finally achieved through an edict in AD 212 by the emperor Caracalla, Roman rule could, to some extent, be legitimised in the eyes of the conquered. This meant that taxes were more easily collected and the need for expensive and uncertain military power reduced. As arguably is the case with some modernist examples of citizenship, such as that associated with the European Union, the status of citizenship became detached from an ethic of participation and was increasingly a thin and legalistic concept, with the largely instrumental motive of undermining sources of social discontent. As Nicolet (1980: 19) contends, in the Roman Empire citizenship meant 'above all, and almost exclusively, the enjoyment of what might be called a right of habeas corpus'. For the vast majority of Roman citizens, citizenship was reduced to a judicial safeguard, rather than a status that denoted political agency. In fact, the concept was stretched to breaking point and citizenship became little more than an expression of the rule of law. In terms of the definition outlined above, Roman imperial citizenship was citizenship in name only. As Derek Heater (1990: 16) observes, the 'Romans [developed] a form of citizenship which was both pragmatic and extensible in application. Yet that very elasticity was the cause ultimately of the perishing of the ideal in its noble form'.

The Roman experience of citizenship retains its interest for at least two reasons. First, it stands as an early example of what Michael Mann (1996) has called in a different context a ruling class strategy to the problem of social order: the idea of citizenship as an expression of common interests, political agency and the fulfilment of human potential is replaced by a somewhat more cynical view of citizenship as an instrument of social control. Second, citizenship in the Roman Empire raises the question of whether a deep sense of citizenship is only possible in a relatively small-scale, homogenous community such as existed in the Greek polis.

After the collapse of the Roman Empire in the West the importance of citizenship diminished even further. In the middle ages, the pursuit of honour through the exercise of citizenship became replaced by the search for personal salvation. In a defining text of the times, Saint Augustine asserted in the *City of God* that individuals should not concern themselves with temporal life and should instead turn inwards to self-contemplation and prayer (Clarke 1994: 62–5). Consequently, the church replaced the political community as the focus for loyalty and moral guidance.

The practice of citizenship did find expression during the medieval period in the context of several European Italian city-republics such as Florence and Venice. Such cities drew inspiration from the republican models of Greece, and particularly Rome. Importantly, they included an ethic of participation, which was lacking in other forms of political community during this period. According to Max Weber (1958: 72), these cities played a crucial role in laying the foundations for the eventual emergence of modern citizenship. Certainly the label Weber applies to these cities – he defines them as a fusion of 'fortress and market' – bears similarities to the context in which modern citizenship emerged. As in the eighteenth and nineteenth centuries, citizenship in the medieval city from the twelfth century onwards was made possible by the development of a money economy and industrial activity that provided the tax base upon which a citizenship community could be constructed. The militia of these cities, like those in America's War of Independence or the citizen army of the French Revolution centuries later, also provided an important sense of obligation and identity for citizens. Moreover, defenders of the autonomy of such political communities, such as Marsilius of Padua, asserted the political, as opposed to sacred, nature of their authority, and thus underlined the essentially secular nature of citizenship (Clarke 1994: 70–3; Heater 1990: 23–4).

However, these cities were exceptions in the context of a feudal system that was 'overwhelmingly princely and hierarchical' (Riesenberg 1992: 187). They also enshrined a citizenship that was non-universal and hierarchical. Most individuals were excluded as a matter of course. Even citizens' rights varied according to property ownership. It is only with the development of liberalism that citizenship was furnished with an egalitarian logic.

CITIZENSHIP AND MODERNITY

Modern notions of citizenship are intimately tied to the development of the liberal state, the foundations of which had been laid by the end of the sixteenth century (Skinner 1978). One of the earliest political theorists to consider the relationship between the individual and political community in this new context was Thomas Hobbes. In perhaps the first work of modern political theory, Hobbes defined the task of his subject as the 'curious search into the rights of states and duties of subjects' (cit. in Skinner 1978a: 349). It is clear from such statements that Hobbes's concern was primarily with issues of security and order, his focus being the rights of the sovereign, not the individual. Hobbes was highly sceptical of participatory theories of citizenship. Indeed, the logic of his theory, which defended the sovereign's right to absolutist power, left little conceptual space for any sense of citizenship. Instead, the obligation to the common interest of the community, associated with citizenship, is replaced by total obedience to the state. The sovereign alone can ensure that anarchy does not destroy the basis for peaceful human interaction. The only 'right' for individuals that Hobbes speaks of is that of self-preservation, which turns out not to be a right in any meaningful sense, since Hobbes accepted that the sovereign shall have power of life and death. Clarke (1996: 53) therefore argues that in Hobbes's theory 'politics and citizenship are terminated' while Weiler (1997: 52) labels Hobbes as the 'father of modern antipolitics'. Hobbes's model for the relationship between the individual and state might, at best, be termed subject-citizenship because it had as its aim the securing of order rather than the performance of civic virtue, or the protection of individual rights.

Yet Hobbes was an important transitionary figure in the history of citizenship, with many of his ideas leading directly to the more developed sense of citizenship found in classical liberals such as Locke. First, unlike in the middle ages, where 'rights and liberties are extended to groups, corporations, estates rather than individual subjects', the individual in Hobbes enjoys a direct relationship with the state which, in practice, increasingly required a more developed sense of citizenship through which this relationship could be mediated (Bendix 1996: 66). Second, Hobbes believed that in terms of their abilities, as well as in their powers to upset the basis of social order, individuals were essentially equal:

Nature hath made men so equall, in the faculties of body, and mind; as that though there bee found one man sometimes manifestly stronger in body, or of quicker mind then another; yet when all is reckoned together, the difference between man, and man, is not so considerable, as that one man can thereupon claim to himselfe any benefit, to which another may not pretend, as well as he.

(Hobbes 1973: 63)

Crucially, this insight enabled liberal thinkers to make the conceptual link between equality and citizenship. Third, and despite Hobbes's personal preference for a monarchical system of government, his theory breaks with the assumption that the ruler and state are indivisible. This meant that in the modern period the state itself, rather than the monarch, became 'the sole appropriate object of its citizens' allegiances' (Skinner 1978: x). Fourth, by arguing that the sovereign should enjoy absolutist power, Hobbes was advocating the concentration of the means of violence. This was important for citizenship since it marked a break with the feudal notion of divided sites of power where violence was exercised by a number of actors. By limiting the exercise of violence to the state in this way, the opportunity was created for more consensual methods of governance to emerge. At the same time, Hobbes's theory of state sovereignty highlights the contradictory relationship between citizenship as consent and the state as the enforcer of order, which, as we shall see in subsequent chapters, had great significance for the context and extent of citizenship.

The liberal tradition founded by Hobbes was developed by Locke, who built upon the idea of the egalitarian individual's direct relationship with the state to construct a rights-based theory of citizenship. Locke's (1924) theory aimed to balance a Hobbesian concern with security with the protection of the rights of life, liberty and property, which for most liberals are the basis for the fulfilment of self-interest. Chapter 3 will explore the limits of these liberal conceptions. However, a philosophical redefinition of citizenship by liberals cannot by itself explain the emergence of modern citizenship. Concrete social changes associated mainly with the transformation of the form of political community meant the status of citizenship began to matter more to those subject to the ever-expanding power of the state. Giddens (1985: 210) expresses this as follows:

> the expansion of state sovereignty means that those subject to it are in some sense – initially vague, but growing more and more definite and precise – aware of their membership in a political community and of the rights and obligations such membership confers.

As the boundaries between states grew more precise, particularly from the eighteenth century onwards, the people within those boundaries became ever more concerned with the conditions of their membership. Mann has called this process 'social caging'. Before the eighteenth century,

> the nature of state elites or of state institutions had mattered little for society. Now they mattered a great deal. The rise of citizenship is conventionally narrated as the rise of modern classes to political power. But classes are not 'naturally political'. Through most of history subordinate classes had been largely indifferent to or had sought to evade states. They were now caged into national organization, into politics, by two principal zookeepers: tax gatherers and recruiting officers.
>
> (Mann 1993: 25)

The political status of citizenship was rendered even more important as the military power and increasingly sophisticated bureaucracy of the state helped undermine competing sites of power. The key to this was the separation of church and state. The bloodshed and subsequent instability caused by the

Reformation led political theorists such as Bodin and Hobbes to look to divorce politics from religion. Political elites shared this view, and the subsequent secularisation of the state following the end of the Wars of Religion in Europe created important space for a secular citizenship to emerge. The Reformation had one further impact upon citizenship. The importance Protestantism placed upon the direct relationship between God and the individual was effectively secularised by Locke into a relationship between the citizen and the state. It is perhaps no coincidence that Hobbes, Marx and Hegel, amongst other modernist thinkers, have therefore drawn comparisons between God and the state, where the state replaces the divine being as the focus of people's aspirations.

One consequence of this much greater power for the state was that the state increasingly became the focal point for demands for the extension of rights. Giddens (1985: 201) terms this process the dialectic of control. By this, Giddens means that although the state's surveillance capabilities over its citizens grew enormously through the development of public education, the courts system, and parliaments, this process of control worked both ways. Greater state power meant that social movements could use the channels of communication created by the state to campaign for rights. For Giddens, the state consequently came to rely more upon consensual means of governance and less on force. Citizenship became an important part of this new system of consensual government, as its extension sought in part to incorporate potentially disruptive groups into the polity. Thus the history of modern citizenship can in part be understood as a series of bargains and trade offs, whereby elites seek to maintain their power through managing the effects of social change and containing the demands of social movements through concessions in the form of rights. This would culminate in the development of social rights, in the form of the welfare state, in many European countries by the middle of the twentieth century.

Some authors such as Mann (1996) and Barbalet (1988) maintain that rights are largely the product of decisions by elites, while others such as Turner (1986) and Giddens (1985) stress the role of social struggle. It seems to me, however, that it is a mistake to try to privilege either struggle or political expediency in the history of citizenship. There are simply too many variables to provide a general theory that can be applied in all places and at all times. What is clear, though, is that the balance of social forces shifted in the modern state compared to those in its absolutist predecessor, which had dominated political life from the fifteenth to the eighteenth centuries. The absolutist states successfully contained demands for rights and maintained subjecthood rather than citizenship as the defining status of their populations. However, the egalitarian logic, which liberalism had injected into citizenship, coupled with the growing importance of the state for people's sense of identity and material needs, was to lead to the creation of what Riesenberg (1992: 1) calls the second citizenship. The coming of modern citizenship cannot then simply be explained in terms of class conflict. Giddens (1985: 208) is right to say that 'class conflict has been a medium of the extension of citizenship rights', but this is only part of the story. The development of citizenship since the eighteenth century has involved conflicts within and between states. Four factors seem to be particularly crucial to explaining the direction of citizenship. The relative significance of these factors has of course varied according to historical circumstances.

First, the struggles of social movements have undoubtedly played an important role in extending citizenship. These have included women, ethnic minorities, and the disabled and sexual minorities, in addition to classes. Second, ideology matters. The universalism of liberalism provided citizenship with an egalitarian potential that excluded groups could draw upon creatively. As Turner (1986: 133) puts it, 'as the waves of citizenship move outwards as a consequence of social movement to achieve real rights, the particularistic criteria which define the person become increasingly irrelevant in the public sphere'. Socialism, which I see as an ideology concerned above all with fulfilling liberalism's promise, is crucial in this regard. In states where socialism has been influential, such as Germany, Sweden and even Britain, social rights, in the form of publicly funded services, have been more extensive than in countries such as the USA, where socialism has been of minimal influence. Nationalism too played a huge role in galvanising support for the extension of rights, being at once a positive and yet limiting force in the history of citizenship. The ambiguous influence of nationalism on citizenship will be discussed in chapter 2.

Third, economic factors, and particularly the triumph of capitalism, are crucial to understanding citizenship. It is not necessary to adopt a Marxist analysis to accept that political elites rely largely upon the performance of the economy. Such elites therefore have a huge personal stake in maintaining the conditions whereby capitalists can prosper. Thus, the needs of the market economy have played a huge part in the form citizenship has taken. A key question, therefore, in the citizenship literature is whether citizenship is opposed to or supportive of capitalism. Marshall (1992), in his influential consideration of this problem, identifies a tension between the egalitarian values of citizenship and the economic inequality that is inherent to capitalism. As a social liberal, who is to some extent aware of the impact such inequalities might have upon social order, and therefore the practice of citizenship, Marshall advocates the use of tax-funded social rights to offset the worst aspects of inequality. The main problem in Marshall's account, however, is that he does not give sufficient consideration to the conditions and interests that sustained social rights in the period he was writing. Marshall's essay was published in 1950, in the infancy of the welfare state in Britain, when social rights appeared irreversible. I consider the problem of social rights in both chapters 3 and 5. Briefly, however, the stage of development that capitalism had reached in the early post-war period was one of mass, Fordist production. This facilitated both high profits and working class organisation. In a classic example of citizenship as social bargain, social rights were largely a concession granted to workers in recognition of workers' ability to exercise trade union power in the workplace (Faulks 1998: 103–7). In the 1980s, the balance of power between labour and capital shifted in favour of the latter. Political elites since then have sought ways to minimise expensive welfare rights in response to calls from capital to cut back on red tape and taxation. The fundamental lesson that can be drawn from the restriction of rights by neo-liberal governments is that while markets can play an important part in promoting individual freedom, economic imperatives cannot take precedence over the political decisions of the community. We cannot allow citizenship to be shaped by the short term, ever-changing imperatives of market forces. This is why in chapter 5 I make the argument for a citizens' income. Like the Greeks, we must recognise the link between material resources and the exercise of citizenship.

Finally, the nature of the liberal state itself is essential to understanding citizenship in modernity. In Table 1.2, I prefaced the term state with the words patriarchal, racialised and capitalist. I have already argued that political elites have more often than not privileged the interests of capital over citizenship. The state, I wish to argue, is also inherently racialised and gendered. This is because the modern state is not, as liberals would have us believe, an essentially neutral political institution. Instead, the state has been fused with a cultural concept of the nation that has been defined in both ethnic and gendered terms. A watershed in the creation of modern citizenship therefore was the French Revolution of 1789 because this event fused state and nation together. Chapter 2 will explore the legacy this revolution has had for citizenship in the form of an analysis of the nation-state.

2

CITIZENSHIP AND THE NATION-STATE

Citizenship in modernity is ambiguous. On the one hand, liberalism, as the dominant ideology of citizenship, has stressed the essentially egalitarian and universal nature of the status. On the other hand, from the eighteenth century onwards, citizenship has been bound closely to the institution of the nation-state and therefore in practice has acted as 'a powerful instrument of social closure' (Brubaker 1992: 23). The extent of citizenship, then, has been determined by boundaries between states, which are both physical and cultural in form. Consequently, citizenship has been about exclusion from, as well as inclusion into the polity. Immigration controls and residency requirements are seen by states as an important part of their sovereignty and represent the material aspects of exclusion. Cultural exclusion has also played its part, in the form of the concept of the nation. This means that individuals within state boundaries, legal residents, guest workers or refugees, as well as foreigners outside state boundaries, can be perceived as 'outsiders' or second-class citizens by the dominant culture of the polity. The two ideas of state and nation, which are the basis for the exclusionary aspects of citizenship, come together in the notion of the nation-state. This fusion is above all a legacy of the French Revolution of 1789, which was to have deep consequences for the future of citizenship.

In this chapter, I begin by exploring the concept of the nation-state as defined by the French Revolution. I will then consider two contrasting perspectives on the appropriate relationship between the nation and citizenship. David Miller (1995) argues that citizenship is an empty idea without its association with the nation. I contend that Miller's defence of nationality is incoherent and that the nation is not an appropriate foundation for citizenship. In opposition to defenders of the nation such as Miller, Oommen (1997) has advanced an interesting thesis to the effect that citizenship must be detached from the cultural idea of nation if it is to serve as an inclusionary concept, capable of uniting diverse groups within increasingly plural societies. The weakness of Oommen's own argument, however, lies in his unwillingness to detach citizenship from the state, as well as the nation. This is because, in his desire to separate state from nation conceptually, Oommen underestimates how the state is in fact inherently racialised and patriarchal. Thus, the state itself, as well as the nation, is a barrier to citizenship. In the final part of the chapter, I suggest that contemporary dilemmas of social membership highlight the contradiction that lies at the heart of the modernist project: the tension between the state as an exclusionary community and citizenship as a universal status.

THE FRENCH REVOLUTION, MODERNITY AND CITIZENSHIP

Before 1789, social membership in France was determined by the pre-modern concepts of subjecthood, hierarchy and domination. Sovereignty, as the determinant of membership, resided in the person of the King, whose authority was underpinned by his claim to represent God on earth. At its outset, what the revolution did was to utilise the concept of the nation in a progressive and secular way: to substitute the monarchy as sovereign with the people as sovereign. In his influential pamphlet *What is the Third Estate?* Sieyès defined the nation as the common people (the Third Estate) who were being denied their rights by the system of aristocracy and monarchy (see Forsyth 1987). Thus the French Revolution, in seeking to implement Sieyès's ideas, was a pivotal moment in the formation of modernity. Rights would no longer be granted to privileged groups only, but instead would reside in the individual citizen in the context of the nation, which represented the will of the people. The centrality of rights was established through the publication of the *Declaration of the Rights of Man and the Citizen* in 1789. This document asserted that 'ignorance, forgetfulness or contempt of the rights of man are the sole causes of public misfortune and governmental depravity' (Waldron 1987: 26–8). The rights enshrined in this document, such as the freedom of speech, worship and justice, were to have a huge influence on radicals throughout Europe who were struggling against privilege to fulfil the potential of the liberal ideas of equality and liberty.

At the heart of the revolution was a new conception of citizenship: one that stressed the universal and egalitarian potential of the status. In the more radical stages of the revolution, however, citizenship also entailed serving the nation, through the performance of civic virtue and military obligation: liberty and equality were to be accompanied by fraternity. The French Revolution was, as Habermas (1974) has noted, therefore more radical in its conception of citizenship than the earlier American Revolution of 1776. The latter was concerned with claiming the rights already owed to Americans through the common law of their colonial masters, the British. It was for this reason that that famous conservative Burke (1968) gave his wholehearted support to the American revolutionaries but not to the French. Burke saw the French Revolution as destroying a noble regime and replacing it with a wholly untried and abstract citizenship. In addition, the French Revolution contained what Burke saw as a dangerous republican element that the American Revolution lacked. As Shklar (1991: 65) puts it: 'The new American citizen was a modern, not a classical, republican . . . not based on virtue, however, but on independent agents and the free play of their interests'. This stress upon individualism resulted largely from the immigrant nature of the American polity. Americans were suspicious of radical politics that might create an oppressive community that would impose the very uniformity from which many Americans had fled in Europe.

In contrast, under the influence of Rousseau's (1968) idea that a community could be united by a 'general will' that transcended social conflict, many of the French revolutionaries saw the revolution as more than the assertion of individual independence through rights and were therefore willing to stress the collectivist aspects of citizenship. They saw a symmetry between the individual and nation, where citizenship would emancipate the individual through obligations as well as through rights. For this reason, Habermas (1974) rejects Marx's claim that citizenship was perceived by the revolutionaries as secondary to purely individual rights of property and contract. Habermas (ibid.: 112) holds that the radicalism of the revolution can be found in its 'idea of a political society, an organisation embracing both state and society'. Certainly, the revolution was no simple assertion of bourgeois freedoms. As Schwarzmantel (1998: 53) argues, commerce was viewed with suspicion by the revolutionaries, who perceived the market's potential for undermining the 'common fabric of citizenship by stressing economic priorities over the will of the people'.

Moreover, at least in the early stages of the revolution, the unity of universal rights and nation were interpreted in an extremely wide and inclusive way. Political rights were extended to foreigners, and honorary citizenship bestowed upon such supporters of the revolution as Thomas Paine and Anarvhisis Cloots. Such inclusiveness did not extend solely to such luminaries. A man from another country could become a French citizen if he had a son born in France, if he owned property within the territory, or was married to a French woman. Brubaker (1992: 7) cites Tallien's comment in 1795 that 'the only foreigners in France are the bad citizens' as an example of how the rights declared in the revolution were intended to reach beyond boundaries of states and to apply to all men regardless of nationality. In support of this interpretation, Silverman (1992: 27) notes how at first national boundaries were left ill defined and the notion of immigrants hardly appeared in the early documents produced by the revolutionaries. Of course, like the citizenship of the pre-modern period, social membership was gendered. The universalism of the revolution was therefore undermined in real terms by its exclusion of women. Nonetheless, even in this regard, the revolution marked a step forward for emancipation generally. As Hunt (1992: 213) comments, 'without the much-maligned universalism of men in 1789, there would have been no demands for inclusion of new groups'.

The more inclusive aspects of citizenship expressed in the revolution were, however, to be undermined by the very circumstances in which they were conceived. Balibar (1994) identifies both internal and external factors that led the revolution towards more exclusive definitions of politics. Externally, the revolutionaries found themselves engaged in a series of wars with reactionary states such as Prussia, Britain and Spain, which were seeking to contain or even destroy the revolution's achievements. Through this experience of violent conflict the idea of nation, and therefore citizenship, became militarised. For example, at the battle of Valmy, fought against the Prussians in 1792, the French troops were heard to cry 'Vive La Nation'. Balibar (ibid.:

53) notes how such events meant that 'the system of fraternity [was] tendentially doubled into a national and, before long, state-centred fraternity'. In the longer term, the French revolutionary wars had the effect of solidifying the boundaries that separated the peoples of Europe, who increasingly came to define themselves in terms of distinct nations.

Internally, the threat of foreign powers, coupled with the inevitable economic problems associated with any revolution, fuelled suspicions within the state between rival factions of revolutionaries. The radicals led by Robespierre and his political group the Montagnards called for a much more inclusive citizenship than had been desired by the earlier liberal revolutionaries. They particularly objected to the division that was made in the 1791 constitution between active and passive citizens. Passive citizens were those workers who could not afford to pay a citizens' tax of at least 3 days' pay and they were denied the opportunity to participate in decision-making processes. Certainly, Robespierre and his fellow revolutionaries' objections to this act of betrayal of the ideals of the revolution were understandable. The notion of a passive citizen, as I have argued in chapter 1, is a contradiction in terms. The problem was that, in the heightened tension of foreign-led counter-revolution, the scene was set for a classic example of what I shall call the republican myth. By this I mean the assertion, in this case through Robespierre's adoption of Rousseau's infamous concept of the general will, that the need for politics can effectively be ended through force of will, or by the inevitable march of history. Following France's defeat by the Austrians at the battle of Neerwinden in 1793, a Committee of Public Safety was set up in April of that year. This became the main instrument of persecution during the period of 1793–94 known as the Great Terror, where thousands lost their lives in the name of the 'true democratic will'. The twisted logic of this episode was expressed by Robespierre when he declared, 'virtue, without which terror is disastrous, and terror, without which virtue is powerless' (Heater 1990: 51).

Heater (1990: 57) argues that the revolution 'politicised the cultural concept of nationality'. This was true in the initial stages of the revolution. However, the violence of the later years of the revolution was to lead to a fusion between nation and state which was to *culturalise* the idea of citizenship and thus confuse the boundaries between citizenship and nationality. The Great Terror also problematised the relationship between citizenship and state. The lesson being that, when tied to the violence of state power, citizenship expressed as the will of the people can easily be mutated into the denial and attempted destruction of difference. This modernist fallacy, the idea that politics can be dispensed with in the name of a final truth, is one of the main attractions of a postmodern citizenship, where rights and responsibilities are seen as methods of managing the inherent and often creative conflicts of society, rather than as a means to transcend such conflict.

The revolution was to end in disaster and many of its more radical achievements were lost in the years of reaction under Napoleon. The confused and contradictory legacy of the revolution nevertheless lived on and indeed increased in intensity as the nineteenth and twentieth centuries saw both the gradual extension of citizenship and the intensification of state boundaries through the deliberate attempt by elites to assert national identity at the expense of the cosmopolitan elements of the French tradition. As Silverman (1992: 6, emphasis added) puts it, France is the 'clearest manifestation of the contradictions in the formation of *all* modern-states'. Given this historical legacy, where citizenship has been tied so closely to the nation-state, the question we need to explore is how necessary or even desirable is this connection?

THE PROBLEM OF THE NATION-STATE

For defenders of national identity, citizenship can only be a meaningful status if connected to the idea of the nation. For Anthony Smith (1995) the nation is the dominant political form of the modern age because it has its roots in collectivities established long before modernity. Citizenship therefore derives its power from the nation-state, which represents 'a sometimes uneasy but necessary symbiosis of ethnic and civic elements' (Smith 1995: 100). Smith is right, it seems to me, on two counts. First, he correctly identifies the inevitable tension within the modern state between two kinds of identity. One is the ethnic and pre-political identity of nationality; the other is the civic, political status of citizenship. Second, he is right to reject the argument that within the context of the state, the two kinds of identity can exist separately: civic nationalism necessarily entails ethnic nationalism to some degree, however much a particular country may claim to embrace only the civic aspects of nationhood. This point is crucial because it implies that if the contradiction (which Smith fully acknowledges and embraces) between the universalism of citizenship and the exclusivity of the nation-state is to be overcome, citizenship must be uncoupled from both nation *and* state. In the rest of this section, I shall mainly be concerned with the relationship between nation and citizenship. My argument will proceed via a critique of Miller's (1995) challenging work on nationality. At the end of this section I will begin to explore the relationship between state and citizenship, as the key to understanding why citizenship has acted as an instrument of closure as well as a status of inclusion. This argument will be pursued throughout the remainder of the book.

Miller (1995) argues that nationality matters because people *believe* that it matters. Any theory of citizenship must therefore recognise this fact, since it is nationality, defined as a shared history, political culture and a common sense of destiny, that provides us with a sense of obligation to our fellow citizens. Without this bond, we are left only with 'strict reciprocity' between self-interested individuals. For Miller, this can only provide for a very weak citizenship and a minimal state: 'Given the possibility of private insurance, we would expect states that lacked a communitarian background such as nationality provides to be little more than minimal states providing only basic security for their members' (ibid.: 72).

There are a number of problems with this argument. First, Miller appears to be arguing that it is axiomatic that the market, in the form of private insurance, is a better provider of people's welfare than any distribution of resources carried out politically, through the decisions of democratic citizens. However, even in the self-interested terms in which Miller couches his argument, collective provision for our needs may well be considered as more efficient. Certainly, Miller advances no evidence to the contrary. Moreover, while it is true that nationality has been an important identity that individuals have often been prepared to privilege over self-interest, it is not the *only* identity that has led to self-sacrifice and altruism. History shows that individuals have been prepared to make the ultimate sacrifice in the name of many causes such as religion, class, gender and the protection of the environment. Less dramatically, Tam (1998: 226) usefully points to the multitude of contexts in which obligations can be generated including cities, regions, unions, professions and clubs. Such bodies often cooperate with similar groups beyond national boundaries, as witnessed in the intensification of cooperation between trade unions throughout Europe recently. What is more, many communities have historically generated high levels of obligation between their members without a notion of nationality. For example, stateless communities such as the American Plains Indians did not need a concept of nation to feel a sense of obligation to each other. To assume, therefore, that we are faced with either a choice of nationality or atomism, and consequently a thin sense of citizenship, is a gross simplification.

Second, when Miller (1995: 59) talks of 'genuine nation-states', he assumes nation-states possess a degree of homogeneity that clearly does not exist anywhere in the world. As Kymlicka

(1995: 1) notes, there are around 600 languages and 5,000 ethnic groups in the world today but only approximately 180 states. This means that in practice all states are in fact multinational, containing as they do many competing cultural and ethnic traditions. At some points in his book, Miller acknowledges that states are invariably multicultural but seems unaware of how this compromises the main tenet of his argument.

The crux of Miller's problem however is this: he appears to assume that nationality is at once a political *and* pre-political idea. On the one hand, he argues that since nationality 'does not require deference to established institutions or the myths that sustain them', it can be inclusive towards new members and tolerant of dissent (Miller 1995: 129–30). This suggests that the form and content of national identity is up for grabs: it can be defined or redefined through dialogue and democratic decision. Miller (ibid.: 181) seems to confirm this highly fluid notion of nationality later in his argument: 'the main elements in the revitalization of nationality will be the same everywhere: an open debate about national identity and its redefinition to accommodate cultural and territorial minorities'. But if nationality is simply to be determined politically, what differentiates it from citizenship? Miller answers this question in a way which contradicts his argument set out in the citations above. He argues that 'there is a sense in which the past always constrains the present: present identities are built out of the materials that are handed down, not started from scratch'. He goes on to state that, in contrast to those who seek to make the form of nationality a matter of choice, 'the nationalist will want to insist that our membership of a national community is not open to choice . . . the public culture which the community embodies forms an unchosen background against which more specific private cultural choices can be made' (Miller 1995: 175, 194). Miller points to how Britain's national identity is deeply rooted in its political culture, established over centuries. But the point is surely that many of the key institutions that make up this culture, such as the monarchy, the House of Lords and the class system, are simply incompatible with, and indeed are in opposition in principle to, Miller's requirement that an 'open debate' be conducted on national identity. An inclusive dialogue on nationality would be likely to dissolve the very institutions upon which British nationality is based! If this were the case, what would be left of nationality? The truth is, Miller cannot have it both ways. Either we are prepared to ring-fence aspects of national identity, protecting it from democratic scrutiny, and thereby preserving many conservative and exclusive institutions and practices, or we embrace citizenship as an identity that privileges politics over culture.

A related problem with Miller's argument is that individuals experience their nationality very differently. Miller makes little reference to the problems of racism, class and gender, and appears to assume that these are but secondary sources of identity that are transcended by the primary identity of nation. This ignores the fact that nation is inherently bound up with gender, class and race. An example of what I mean has been provided in an excellent analysis of gender and nation by Yuval-Davis (1997). She argues that women have a very different relationship to national discourses than men. Women's relationship to nation is not only different from men's, however, it is also unequal. For example, men are seen as the defenders of the nation, as illustrated by the obligation for men to undertake military duty, whereas women are seen as reproducers of the nation through their role as mothers and carers. Thus, women's right to bodily integrity is often challenged by nationalist discourses that demand that women reproduce at a certain rate for the good of the nation. In Japan during the 1930s, for instance, Japanese women were pressured to breed for the greater good of the empire. In Britain, when Beveridge was putting together his 1942 report upon which the welfare state was to be based, he defended a gendered and unequal form of welfare by arguing that married women did not need the same access to unemployment benefit as men because women had 'other duties' (Lowe 1993: 33). Women have also been seen as symbols of the nation that need to be defended, rather than active participants: 'gendered bodies and sexuality play pivotal roles as territories, markers and reproducers of the narratives of nations . . . women, in their "proper" behaviour, their "proper" clothing, embody the line which signifies the collectivity's boundaries' (Yuval-Davis, 1997: 38). Because Miller ignores such inequalities, he defends a citizenship that is undercut by the pathologies of national sentiment; a sentiment that inevitably is defined in the interests of male, white and privileged elites.

Interesting research by Hall (1994) into the passage of the 1867 Reform Act in Britain, which extended political rights to between 35 and 40 per cent of adult, male workers, has found that the debate in Parliament and amongst the political elite generally was concerned with the extent to which the proposed extension of citizenship would undermine the fabric of the nation. One contributor in the House of Commons concluded that the extension of rights to heads of household would not 'make us any less English, or less national, than we are now' (Hall 1994: 19). Nevertheless, it was felt that the inclusion of women would subvert women's 'natural' role and undermine the nation. Around the time of these debates in Parliament the issue of political autonomy in Jamaica was also discussed. However the liberal, Lord Grey felt that 'from all the evidence I have been able to collect, I have come to the conclusion that for many years to come the Negroes will be unfit to exercise political power' (ibid.: 22). Even progressive MPs such as J. S. Mill supported this line. Indeed, in his famous tract *On Liberty*, Mill (1974) declared that liberty was for 'civilised' nations only, thus reflecting a common liberal trait of defending citizenship at home and despotism abroad without any sense of contradiction. As Hall (1994: 29) concludes, the Victorian idea of nation 'derived its particular and concrete meaning from Empire'. The Reform Acts in Britain gradually weakened the link between formal citizenship and class but as Hall (ibid.: 29) comments, 'property was no longer the basis of the suffrage, but "race", gender, labour and the level of civilisation now determined who was included in and excluded from the political nation'. In summary, then, the very constitution of nation is bound up with deep social divisions that definitions of nation still perpetuate today.

Finally, Miller (1995: 80) necessarily embraces an exclusive and statist concept of citizenship. He argues for instance that 'we are not in most cases required by justice to intervene to safeguard the human rights of foreigners'. Miller thereby appears to support the argument, long established in the realist school of international relations, that order and justice are mutually exclusive goals (Bull 1977). Miller argues that to stretch our obligations beyond our own nation would be to risk their very existence, founded as they are upon the doctrine of state sovereignty. As I shall elaborate in chapter 6, this is to deny three things about the dynamic character of citizenship.

First, citizenship is a momentum concept that must be expanded beyond the state to be truly secure. What I mean by this is that to deny others basic rights that we enjoy on the grounds that they are culturally different is to put at risk our own rights and the basis of social order. A second, and closely related argument, is that with the intensification of globalisation, the basis of social order in any single community cannot be safeguarded by that community alone. The rise of global risks has rendered boundaries between states uncertain. Many of the problems that threaten the benefits of citizenship can therefore only be tackled through a global approach to governance. Nationalities are often described as communities of fate, but now, more than ever, our fates are intimately linked to those of other communities. Third, the obligations of citizenship require that we take our responsibility to other communities seriously. Many of the roots of global problems today, such as the debt crisis, global poverty and environmental damage, are to be found in the self-interested activities of Western states. Thus our sense of citizenship demands that we develop obligations towards those who have lost out in the unequal neo-liberal order constructed in the interests of Western states.

For these reasons, I find the arguments of nationalists such as Miller unconvincing. At the time of the French Revolution, it may have been that the nation was a useful tool through which privilege could be undermined and a more egalitarian citizenship developed. Although as Habermas (1994: 22) reminds us, the very origin of the word nation is the Roman word *natio* which was used to refer to 'peoples and tribes who were not yet organised into political associations'. Today it is becoming clear that the idea of nation is increasingly a barrier rather than a supporting pillar of citizenship. For this reason, in a perceptive analysis, Oommen (1997) seeks to separate rather than celebrate the relationship between nation and citizenship.

Oommen contends that to understand citizenship we must first uncouple nation from the state. Nation is defined by Oommen as the fusion of territory and language and is therefore a cultural, and I would say pre-political status. By pre-political I mean that the form and membership of the nation are determined by geography and history, not by democratic deliberation. The state, on the other hand, is essentially a legal concept. Oommen (1997: 136) considers the fusion of these two ideas, in the form of the nation-state, as 'an unfortunate aspiration, which was never realized even in Western Europe'. As we have already noted, the conflation of state and nation led to citizenship increasingly being confused with nationality and thereby attaining a cultural as well as political status. Instead of acting as an inclusive concept, which could bind people from different cultural backgrounds together, citizenship has been racialised and therefore rendered exclusive in a similar way to nationality.

Oommen (ibid.: 21–2) argues that 'identity based on nationality and ethnicity will not be eclipsed by modernization, as contemporary polities are increasingly becoming hetero-geneous due to migration'. If we are to make ordered and just societies out of the plural mix that are modern states it is therefore essential, argues Oommen, that we make use of the egalitarian aspirations of citizenship and distance the concept from that of nation. In this account, 'the very idea of homogenous nation-states ought to be abandoned' (Oommen 1997: 202). We cannot reasonably expect minorities to become nationals or to assimilate culturally. Instead, we must separate nationality from citizenship and citizen status should be granted according to residence rather than cultural integration and naturalisation. This would have the effect of eroding the stigma of minority status and would enhance the opportunity these groups have to participate in the wider society. Thus, the whole of the com-munity would be enriched by the influx of new approaches to politics provided by minorities. To avoid the problem of majority resentment however, Oommen claims that it is necessary to insist upon minorities fulfilling obligations well as receiving rights. Oommen is surely correct to argue that residency rather than nationality must determine citizenship. Current confusions in Europe and elsewhere over the relationship between nation and citizenship support Oommen against the arguments of national-ists like Miller. Before I explore some of these issues, I would like at this stage to raise one problem with Oommen's analysis which will be revisited particularly in chapter 6.

Oommen (ibid.: 228) argues that citizenship is meaningless outside the context of the state: 'to dissociate citizenship from its very source – the state – is to render the notion irrelevant and meaningless'. It is here that Oommen's sharp distinction between state and nation runs into trouble: it ignores the intimate connection historically between the state and nation. In reality, once the state's boundaries began to strengthen, the state's claim over the monopoly of force became more credible, and the cosmopolitan aspects of the French Revolution had subsided in their influence, the development of some cultural method for legitimising the state power seemed inevitable. The idea of nation provided such an identity and cannot be understood as an independent variable in the way Oommen suggests.

As Smith (1995) has argued, the idea of nation is to some extent rooted in pre-modern identities. More importantly, though, it is connected to the bureaucratic and economic revolutions associated with the development of the modern state (Calhoun 1997). First, the growth in the state's surveillance and administrative capacities led the state to classify residents in terms of insiders and outsiders in the interest of determining such resources as tax liability and military duty, thus drawing important distinctions between nationals and foreigners. Second, nationality provided a supportive context for state-led industrial policies, which would give political elites the economic power through which overseas markets and resources could be won. That is to say that industrial capitalism and class relations developed in the context of the state (Mann 1993). Industrial capitalism both required and in turn encouraged a degree of cultural homogeneity to provide stable consumer and labour market patterns. Third, nationality was actively encouraged by elites through public education, rituals, anthems, flags and other symbols of unity, which sought to develop allegiance to the state. This loyalty was needed to offset potentially destabilising social divisions such as class conflict, and to ensure unity amongst citizens in times of crisis such as war.

Consequently, it is not just the nation that is a barrier to the emancipatory potential of citizenship, it is also the state. To separate nation and state in the way that Oommen attempts is to miss the interdependent relationship between the two in practice. Moreover, if citizenship is defined purely in statist terms, as Oommen argues it should be, the problems of ethnic minorities, or indeed any other disadvantaged group, will remain unresolved. This is because the coercive power of the state will always be wielded in the interests of the dominant cultural group and will prevent the kind of resolution to conflict that Oommen believes will result from the extension of citizenship to cultural minorities.

CONTEMPORARY DILEMMAS OF STATE MEMBERSHIP

As Oommen contends, in the modern world it is indeed states that confer nationality. In practical terms, because the state is the pre-eminent institution of governance, the state also grants the citizen rights and obligations. The determination of nationality is normally settled in two ways: through birth within the state's territory or through descent via one's parents. Most states mix the two systems and allow various degrees of flexibility in naturalising residents who wish to change their nationality. It has become common place, however, to contrast Germany and France as examples of the two systems. Brubaker (1992: x) is the best example of this argument. He contends that in France nationality is 'defined expansively, as a territorial community', whilst Germany is a 'community of descent'. According to this view then, France represents the progressive modernist approach to social membership, which is political more than it is cultural; the key to membership in France being the acceptance of its secular republican values on the part of would be citizens. These values are said to transcend particularities such as race or religion. Germany, in contrast, has stressed ties of blood rather than political commitment when defining legitimate membership of the nation: citizenship is tied closely to ethnic origin. This has created much controversy since it has led to the bizarre situation whereby, following the collapse of communist rule across Eastern Europe, many 'ethnic' Germans, who in fact could not speak German, and who knew little of its culture, were welcomed into

Germany as citizens coming home. For example, in 1994 alone, 222,591 Eastern Europeans were welcomed 'back' into Germany as citizens. In contrast, the 2 million Turkish guest workers, who have often lived in Germany for years and who pay taxes, run businesses and form part of a thriving multicultural Germany, are denied citizenship (Migration News 1998). This example of the experience of migrant workers is just one of many contemporary dilemmas that are highlighting the contradictions of the fusion of citizenship, state and nation. The question of immigration is complicated by fears of economic globalisation, which demands ever-more cost cutting and deregulation, and therefore appears to challenge the foundations of welfare rights. Thus the question of migrants, whether they be refugees fleeing from oppression in Africa, Asia or Yugoslavia, or temporary guest workers, has become merged with the question of economics: how can the basis of the citizenship community be maintained if the demands for expensive rights are increased in this way? However, rarely is this question asked in such a rational, calm way. Instead, questions of social membership within industrial societies are raised in emotive terms that prevent a clear line being drawn between the 'progressive' French system on the one hand and the racialised German system on the other. The sharp contrast Brubaker draws between the two systems is therefore overstated. Silverman's (1992) analysis is closer to reality when he argues that the French and German cases are different expressions of the modernist contradictions of citizenship. The key to understanding the current situation is, as Silverman contends, to recognise that in the nineteenth century, the nation-state effectively hijacked the concept of citizenship. What this meant is that, in the context of the state, citizenship and nation cannot be conceptually or practically divorced from discourses of race, ethnicity and therefore racism and exclusion. As Silverman (1992: 26) comments, 'racism is not an external evil which periodically plagues the body politic; it is an integral part of the very constitution of modern nation-states'. Through cultivating nationalist sentiment, and by linking this sentiment to definitions of citizenship, political elites have often drawn upon the exclusive aspects of citizenship rather than its emancipatory potential.

A recent example that highlights these unfortunate connections between citizenship and ethnicity, and that calls into question arguments of nationalists such as Miller, is the 'headscarf affair' in France, which began in 1989. Silverman (1992: 1) rightly identifies this affair as representing a 'crisis of the nation-state', for it shows how even in the country that prides itself upon its love of politics over divisive cultural identities, the assumptions that underpin 'legitimate membership' are deeply racialised. The affair began when three female Muslim students attended their school in the town of Creil wearing headscarves. This seemingly minor incident triggered an astonishing, somewhat pathological reaction, across France, when the school sent the three girls home, having decided that their actions represented an ostentatious expression of a particularistic identity, which was at odds with the nation's emphasis upon transcendent republican values. There ensued a public debate dissecting the nature of social membership in France. Latent fears about the influx of fundamentalist Islam surfaced and leading republicans rejected calls from 'multiculturalists' such as the anti-racist group SOS Racisme who initially defended the rights of the girls to wear the headscarf in school. Leading intellectuals, amongst them Regis Debray and Alain Finkielkraut, wrote an open letter to the *Nouvel Observateur* asking whether the affair would prove to be 'the Munich of republicanism' if the government compromised its republican values. The affair was part of wider anxieties over immigration and its apparent threat to republicanism and was conducted against a background of rising support for the *Front National* of Le Pen, the extreme right wing party that has won up to 15 per cent of the vote in national elections in France and has gained control of several local authorities. The election of a conservative government in 1993 led to a hardening of government attitudes towards naturalisation and the 1993 Pasqua laws tightened considerably the criteria for the granting of French citizenship to foreign residents or would-be migrants. The irony of all of this is that the allegedly inclusive language of republicanism was used to justify exclusionary practices against outsiders. Silverman (1992: 15) captures these contradictions well in a memorable passage:

> Immigration can represent both the liberal republic and the threat to the liberal republic; it is the embodiment of France's capacity for assimilation and proof of a break-down in assimilation; it is the embodiment of pluralism and proof of the impossibility of pluralism.

Behind the language of neutrality espoused by the republican tradition, there are all kinds of cultural assumptions that make difficult, if not impossible, the very assimilation that republican citizenship demands. For example, although ethnic origin is not officially recognised in France, terms like French Muslims are frequently used by officials, are often the basis for housing allocations, and are also used in the management of other local services. The official denial of such categories by the authorities can and does result in the problems of immigration being depoliticised and thereby being 'solved' by the bureaucracy, rather than through democratic methods. The idea of a secular France, which denies religious particularity, is also largely a myth. Taxpayers in fact do contribute to the running of Catholic schools and churches. In addition, the focus upon Islam, expressed in the headscarf affair, ignored the fact that pupils may wear crucifixes or 'I love Jesus' shirts without risk of sanction.

The assertion of republicanism in the face of a wealth of evidence to suggest that citizenship is linked closely to a racialised nationality is to misunderstand the roots of the alienation felt by minorities in France. Balibar (1991: 16) believes the key to the contradictions of modern citizenship can be found in the state, which he defines as

> an administrative, police and judicial apparatus designed to protect one part of the population while increasing the risks for another part, without it ever being possible to draw clearly, at the necessary place, the demarcation line between the two 'groups' or 'populations'.

The state, through its efforts to create unity and symmetry between citizens, necessarily denies and suppresses difference. Paradoxically, the state attempts to achieve homogeneity by stigmatising and accenting the very differences it wishes to deny. As Balibar (1991: 15) observes, 'minorities only exist in actuality from the moment when they are codified and controlled'. The state's supposed neutrality in much social science literature masks the state's origins in the exclusion of the 'other': the boundaries of the state only make sense when those who are 'outside' those boundaries are immutably different. Moreover, in the context of the colonial history of countries like France, ideas of difference have often been mixed with ideas of superiority. It is no coincidence, for example, that it was at the height of imperialism in the nineteenth century that 'race science' developed, whereby colonial dominance by the French in Algeria for instance could be justified through the spurious logic of racial superiority. The work of feminists like Yuval-Davis (1997), discussed above, also shows that supposed state neutrality hides the patriarchal assumptions that shape men and women's very different relationship to the state.

Debates over the management of the 'problem' of minorities in France have missed the connection between a state-centred definition of citizenship and the exclusion of these minorities.

The hysterical reaction in France to the 'threat' of fundamentalist Islam is symptomatic of a deeper sense of crisis within the nation-state. As Favell (1997: 10) argues, the fear is that immigration 'might expose the fragility of other social and political ties that keep the whole nation together'. Too often the proposed solution to these problems has been to tighten the controls on immigration into the polity, while at the same time insisting that those 'outsiders' who do remain integrate fully into the dominant culture. The problem with this strategy is first that restrictive approaches to immigration threaten the civil rights of those immigrants who are allowed to remain but who through the colour of their skin or their cultural practices can be easily identified as standing outside of the dominant culture. Legal residents may therefore be subject to scrutiny by the authorities that seek to enforce their restrictive immigration policies. This in turn makes minorities feel less part of the culture that they are supposed to be unifying with. Second, such policies deny the positive effect immigrants can have on the host culture, importing new talents, tastes and resources and thereby enriching the whole community.

Third, a developed sense of citizenship demands that each citizen develops empathy and understanding for other cultures and sensitivity to the interests and needs of others. A diverse, rather than homogenous polity is much more likely to create the opportunity for the skills of empathy and sympathy to develop (Clarke 1996: 59). Diversity also provides the polity with a positive critique of its institutions, which is vital if such institutions are to remain responsive and dynamic. As Kostakopoulou (1998: 898) contends:

> Acknowledging the particularistic anchoring of constitutional principles . . . is a good reason to expose them to critical exchanges by other interpretative communities, not to insulate them from the very forces and challenges that could allow them

to operate in a more universalist context. Critical exchanges and collisions enhance the possibility for reflective self-awareness by showing the limits and relativity of one's political culture. Exposure of the limits leads to a better understanding of the whole and its potential. A strong democracy needs a strong critique.

A positive acknowledgement of the contribution that immigrants make, and the empathy that might be generated through such a positive approach is also connected to the need for citizens to embrace obligations that reach beyond their immediate locality. It is in the interest of good citizenship that Dauenhauer (1996: 185) argues that immigration from non-democratic societies should be prioritised by democratic systems of government, as a method of promoting the spread of democratic citizenship globally.

Fourth, by focusing anxieties over the future of the nation-state upon immigration and minorities, the danger is that the roots of social division, such as poverty, discrimination, and racism are left untackled. There is little doubt that the 'immigration problem' can be a useful diversionary tactic used by politicians in their efforts to avoid addressing more fundamental problems with the economic and political structures of liberal democracies. The danger with the abstract republican approach to citizenship in France is that demands to reform the context of citizenship to make the status meaningful for minorities are set aside and replaced by simple-minded calls for integration into what is in reality an often hostile and racist polity. Contrary to the claims of nationalists such as Miller (1995), the inherently cultural and pre-political idea of the nation is an inappropriate basis for citizenship. When allied to the coercive force of the state, national discourses of citizenship serve only to suppress difference and prevent the development of a sense of mutual obligations amongst immigrant and host populations alike. The commitment to abstract republican citizenship in France highlights the fact that, even in a seemingly progressive state, citizenship is undermined by its connection with cultural essentialism. By this I mean a defence of cultural identity that is closed and hostile to minorities.

For this reason, Habermas (1994) advances an alternative basis for citizenship, which he calls constitutional patriotism. What this refers to is the development of a sense of obligation between members of a polity which is a strictly political, not cultural entity. Borders are for administrative purposes only, and are not used to denote the boundary point where obligations end and suspicion begins. The challenge of constitutional patriotism is to engender amongst citizens a commitment to their institutions of government, without having to rely on a spurious cultural unity. This suggests a polity where boundaries are fluid, not fixed. As Kostakopoulou (1998: 897) notes, how we perceive borders and the role they play in human interaction is crucial to the nature of citizenship: 'conceiving community in terms of the nation state [is to project] boundaries as barriers (stopping points) and not as permeable membranes (meeting points)'.

Democracy is crucial to constitutional patriotism. The community makes its own future through deliberation rather than through reference to the past and some mythical sense of a shared fate as a nation; design rather than destiny is the guiding principle of constitutional patriotism. Indeed, as I shall argue in chapter 5, it is only by reforming the institutions that facilitate political participation that the conflicts between individuals and groups, between dominant and marginal cultures, can be managed. Constitutional patriotism also entails a community that does not seek to unify its identity by denying the identities of minorities or outsiders: it is citizenship without enemies.

The only appropriate criteria for social membership in a polity run on the principles of constitutional patriotism is therefore that of residence. It may be appropriate to limit membership according to the practicalities of administration but the key is that if citizenship is uncoupled from the exclusionary discourses of the nation-state, there is a much greater chance of citizens realising that their obligations necessarily reach beyond their immediate locality. This will almost certainly mean not only more fluid political boundaries but also a proliferation of what Heater (1990) usefully refers to as multiple citizenship. Individuals will increasingly have multiple sites through which to exercise their obligations and rights and these would include the neighbour-hood, the associations of civil society, local, regional and federal government and more global bodies such as a reformed and enhanced United Nations (Held 1995). If citizenship is concerned with the interdependence between the individual and the community, then we must recognise that globalisation has changed the nature and focus of that interdependence. As Waldron (1992: 771) insists, 'the full extent of human interdependence is now global, not national'.

The central argument of this chapter has been that the legacy of the French Revolution for citizenship has been a confused and contradictory one. Initially, the ideas of citizenship promoted in the revolution were largely progressive, inclusive, political and cosmopolitan. The experience of war and the violent radicalism of extremist republicans, who in fact sought not the fulfilment of citizenship but its negation and replacement by a mythical and oppressive notion of the general will, helped to fuse citizen-ship with a racialised and gendered notion of the nation. I have argued against Miller's celebration of nationality as the foundation stone of citizenship and agreed with Oommen that citizenship must be uncoupled from this regressive concept if it is to fulfil its emancipatory potential. The contradictory legacy of modernity is perhaps most clearly visible in France today, with the stress it places upon republican citizenship at odds with the reality of a pluralist and divided society. The contemporary dilemma of social membership, which the French experience highlights well, is that globalisation is making the boundaries upon which the state has relied increasingly uncertain. This is why Habermas is surely right to argue that an important step towards managing the problems of increasingly heterogeneous polities is to make citizenship a strictly political concept, separate from the confusion and uncertainty of culture, ethnicity or nation.

I go on to suggest in chapter 6, however, that globalisation is making the connection between citizenship and the state as untenable as the relationship between citizenship and nationality. As I have argued, in historical and conceptual terms, the ideas of state and nation have been intimately connected: the formation of the former demanded the promotion of the latter. Before I address this question of how globalisation is transforming the nature of citizenship, I need first to explore the content of citizenship. As Oommen suggests, ensuring that all citizens, regardless of their nationality or ethnicity, are granted rights and fulfil their responsibilities is crucial to maintaining social cohesion. Citizenship, in whatever political context it is exercised, will consist of a package of rights and responsibilities. The next three chapters connect the question of the content of citizenship with the questions of its context, extent and depth. In chapter 4, I look at whether social differences between men and women and between different ethnic groups prevent the attainment of a common citizenship that is universal. Chapter 5 explores ways in which rights and responsibilities and the relationship between them can be enhanced and intensified. First, however, I will explore whether the tension identified by liberalism between different types of rights and between rights and responsibilities is inherent to the practice of citizenship.

3

RIGHTS AND
RESPONSIBILITIES

A controversial debate in citizenship theory concerns the appropriate content of the status in terms of the rights and responsibilities that it bestows. Are different kinds of rights, in particular civil and social rights, contradictory principles? Are rights and responsibilities mutually dependent, or does an emphasis on one undermine the other? Our thinking on these questions has been dominated by the liberal tradition, which undoubtedly has had most influence of any ideology upon the practice of citizenship in Western society. Theoretically it is through a dialogue with liberalism that alternative radical and conservative perspectives have been formulated.

This chapter will therefore begin by exploring liberalism. I will argue that while liberalism has many strengths, in particular its emphasis upon citizenship as a collection of equal rights, its emancipatory potential is undermined by its assumptions concerning the relationship between the individual and the community and between the market and politics. In the first section, I set out the core set of values that underpin liberal conceptions of citizenship. I will draw upon traditions, such as feminism and Marxism, to construct a critique of liberal citizenship that identifies liberalism as a dualistic theory that presupposes a tension between the individual and community. From this 'primary dualism', a series of related problems can be derived. One of these liberal dualisms is the apparent opposition between rights and responsibilities. For many critiques, the substance of citizenship has been seriously damaged by liberalism's emphasis upon individual rights. Instead, it is argued by conservatives and communitarians that we must insist on greater duties and obligations. In the second section, I consider some of these arguments. However, as I argue in the final section, what is required for a coherent theory of citizenship is that the false opposition between rights and responsibilities be dissolved.

THE LIMITS OF LIBERAL RIGHTS

In the liberal tradition, citizenship is defined primarily as a set of individual rights. These rights are said to serve several functions. Most importantly, the possession of rights denotes individual autonomy. Rights give space to the individual to develop their interests and fulfil their potential free from interference from other individuals or from the community as a whole. The first liberal theorists to assign a central role to rights, such as Locke and Paine, believed that the citizen needed to be protected from the growing power of the state. Without the civil rights of life, liberty and property, the individual would always be at the mercy of arbitrary political power. While the classical liberals of the seventeenth and eighteenth centuries felt the state was required to maintain order, it was in the words of Paine, a necessary evil. Moreover, classical liberals contended that individuals were rational and self-determining *before* the formation of the state. The basis, then, for the authority of the state is a contract between autonomous actors. The individual consents to give up some liberties in return for the security that the state can offer. This abstract individualism means that liberals understand the individual and community as being in opposition and, as we shall see, in part this explains their ambivalence towards responsibilities, democracy and social rights. The implications for citizenship of these liberal assumptions are expressed in Figure 3.1.

Individual	Community
Agency	Structure
Private sphere	Public sphere
Men as citizens	Women as carers
Freedom through the market	Equality through politics
Market rights	Social rights
Active citizens	Passive citizens
Rights	Responsibilities/democracy
Sovereignty	Human rights
Science	Nature

Figure 3.1 Ten dualisms of liberal citizenship

The emphasis liberals place upon individual autonomy makes them suspicious of notions of community. The fear is that the community will seek to impose obligations upon the individual that constrain or contradict his or her self-interest. This stands in direct contrast to the holistic approach of the ancient Athenian polis. In the polis, the idea of the individual having a meaningful existence outside of the community was unthinkable. The needs of the community and the interests of the citizen were seen as indivisible. Thinkers who have drawn inspiration from ancient, more participatory models of citizenship have helped expose the incoherence of liberalism. Both socialists and republicans are attracted by the thick conception of citizenship associated with the polis and see the citizenship of liberalism as an impoverished alternative. Liberalism's dualistic approach to citizenship has also drawn criticisms from feminists, postmodernists and ecologists who discern the damaging implications of its assumptions for human relations and the natural environment.

A closely related dichotomy to that of the individual and community is that of agency and structure. Because liberals start with the assumption that the individual is a rational, atomistic actor, they tend towards agency-centred explanations of human behaviour: we shape our own lives through the choices we make. Rights facilitate these choices. The problem with this is that it assumes a very one-dimensional understanding of power. To the liberal mind, power is an individual capacity that is used intentionally and for a clear purpose. This ignores the nature of constraints that structures of power such as race, class and gender place upon the individual. Inequalities associated with the class system, patriarchy and racism are deeply rooted in society and are crucial to understanding why the formal rights of citizenship are not effective for some groups. An illustration of the way inequalities of power are woven into the fabric of social life, and cannot therefore be reduced to rational choice, is captured in the notion of institutional racism. In 1993, the black teenager Stephen Lawrence was murdered by a gang of white youths in southeast London. The subsequent investigation by the Metropolitan Police failed to bring the killers to justice and was viewed by the Lawrence family and civil rights activists as grossly incompetent. A public investigation into the affair found that the police were guilty of 'institutional racism', which the inquiry's report defined as 'an unwitting and unconscious prejudice against ethnic minorities' (Johnston et al. 1999). This particular case is extremely unusual in that we find a rare acceptance by the establishment that structures of power operate in such a way as to deny some people their basic rights.

The way that inequalities shape the practice of citizenship can be further illustrated by a consideration of the public–private divide, which liberals defend. In liberal theory, market interactions and the pursuit of personal interest characterise the private realm. Civil rights protect this sphere from interference from the public realm. Liberals are therefore keen to justify such rights as liberty and property in the strongest terms. Locke (1924) for example considered such rights as natural. By this, he meant that men (not women) possessed rights that were inalienable and could not be taken away by any political authority. The public realm was to serve the interests of individuals and to provide defence and security for private interactions. There is no necessary connection between liberalism and democracy because as long as the sovereign, whether it be a monarchy or democracy, does not seek to undermine civil rights, then its rule can be seen as legitimate. However, as the economic power of the capitalist class grew in the eighteenth and nineteenth centuries, the bourgeoisie demanded political rights as well. These were initially extended to property owners who sought to oversee the protection of their possessions by controlling the state through political representation.

Feminist commentators have exposed the apparent neutrality of the public–private divide as a sham. In fact, the 'freedom' of the private sphere is premised upon a highly unequal relationship between men and women. Virtually all prominent liberal commentators have a gendered view of citizenship. Thus, Paine believed that the only natural inequality with humanity was between the sexes, while Locke describes man as the 'master' of his family (Faulks 1998: 25–7). Social liberals like Marshall and Green also either ignore important differences between the experiences of men and women, or seek to naturalise those differences. For example, T. H. Green attacks the practice of polygamy as an infringement of the right 'of the wife, who is morally lowered by exclusion from her *proper position in the household* and by being used, more or less, as the mere instrument of the husband's pleasure' (Green 1986: 185, emphasis added). Green assumes that monogamous marriage is a condition of women's morality. Moreover, he considers men to be the rightful heads of their households and therefore a woman's position within the family, as well as in the public sphere, is inherently subordinate to that of her husband. It is clear, then, that women are not considered by Green to be rational political agents, capable of practising citizenship. Such patriarchical attitudes pervade liberalism and make a mockery of the alleged neutrality of the public–private divide.

Pateman (1988), in a perceptive critique of liberalism, argues that the social contract that classical liberals see as forming the basis of political authority, is in fact built upon a predetermined sexual contract. The use of the term contract in this context is somewhat misleading since the source of male power is violence and the oppression of women. There is, therefore, no sense of agreement on behalf of women. Nonetheless, the thrust of Pateman's argument is insightful. In liberalism, men are seen as political and economic actors, whereas women are seen as carers rather than citizens. Patriarchal attitudes run through the history of political thought and clearly are not confined to the liberal tradition (Coole 1993). However, this blatant inequality is particularly hard to justify through liberal principles. This highlights the crucial importance of the liberal doctrine of equality discussed in chapter 1. It is only with the development of liberal ideals that patriarchy and other restrictive structures of power could begin to be challenged. Walby (1990) has developed this point in her discussion of the transition from private to public patriarchy. Walby shows how, partly through the expanding power of the state, and partly because of the struggles of women themselves, women have managed to gain greater access to the workplace and political institutions, particularly in the twentieth century. In a private system of patriarchy, through their control of economic and political institutions, and as 'masters' of their families, men are able to dominate the women in their lives very effectively. With the onset of public patriarchy, the ideals of citizenship now begin to be extended to women and enhance the opportunities women have to develop separate economic and political lives. The public profile of women has undoubtedly increased in the twentieth century and this marks a considerable progression. However, women are still very much under-represented in the most important positions of power. It is, therefore, a mistake to draw too sharp a distinction between these forms of patriarchy since it is true, as Walby's own work shows, that women still lack important rights and suffer from oppression. As Lister (1997) has argued, for citizenship to have greater meaning for women, we must address the problem of how the egalitarian values of citizenship can be translated into the personal relationships of the private sphere, and how the resources can be made available to enable women to participate fully as citizens, free from the unequal burden of care for children and other dependants. The crucial point is, however, that the ideal of equality, so central to the liberal tradition, has been essential in providing the impetus towards greater opportunities for women.

The public–private divide is also central to socialist critiques of liberal citizenship. Marx's (1994) essay *On the Jewish Question* remains the most penetrating. The key to understanding this divide is to consider liberalism's perspective on the fifth dualism in Figure 3.1 (see page 57), namely the relationship between equality and liberty. For Marx, the liberal doctrine of equality is important but limited. This is because in the liberal state, individuals are considered equal only in the public sphere, when they are participating politically as citizens. In their private lives, as workers or capitalists, individuals are subject to the market laws of supply and demand, which liberals consider the most effective method for generating prosperity and distributing resources. These market interactions inevitably result in serious inequalities that, for Marx, undermine the significance of formal rights. What does it mean to have civil rights if one is subject to job insecurity, exploitation or the threat of unemployment due to a downturn in the economic cycle? Thus, for Marx, citizenship in its liberal form represents a false universalism that masks the real sources of domination.

It is true that liberals are sceptical about the role politics can play in determining the distribution of resources. The market is seen as the true guarantor of individual freedom. The conditions of a market economy, particularly private property, must therefore be protected through civil rights. This is why classical liberals seek to naturalise civil rights and treat them as existing prior to the formation of the state. In effect, liberals seek to restrict the legitimate scope of democratic decisions. Even radical liberals like J. S. Mill (1974: 62) were wary of the extension of political rights to the masses in the nineteenth century. Mill feared the development of a 'tyranny of the majority' where the masses would impose restrictions upon the liberties of the private sphere. As Marshall (1992: 25) contends, 'the political rights of citizenship, unlike civil rights, were full of potential danger to the capitalist system'.

Neo-liberals, such as Hayek (1944), are more intense than Mill in their hostility to political rights. Because Hayek believes that the inequalities of the private sphere are both inevitable and desirable, he considers democracy to be at best a utilitarian device that should be limited strictly to those areas of life that cannot be determined by market forces. Nozick (1974) goes even further. Any attempt to seek social justice through the practice of democratic citizenship is an infringement of civil rights. Therefore the state should act as a night-watchman, providing security, but in the most inconspicuous way possible. The state should not concern itself with the material welfare of its citizens since this would inevitably mean the state interfering in the distribution of resources that is best determined by the market.

As much as political rights present a potential challenge to the market dominance liberals defend, it was with the development of social rights in the twentieth century in many liberal states that citizenship began to pose a potential challenge to the imperatives of the market. Social rights include income support, state-funded education and public health. Because they are funded through taxation, social rights appear to stand in tension with civil rights and in particular the right to property. Marshall (1992) considered the development of social rights, which were institutionalised principally through the creation of the welfare state, as having the potential to significantly modify the capitalist system and to offset some of the negative aspects of market inequalities. This is why the social liberalism of Marshall should be considered a step forward for citizenship. Unlike the classical liberals, Marshall was able to discern the limiting effects of capitalism upon citizenship. However, Marshall, like all liberals, is a firm supporter of the market economy and in later writings came to the view that social rights had been detrimental to important freedoms symbolised by civil rights (Rees 1995). With this observation, Marshall expresses a common theme in liberal- ism concerning the inherent tension between different kinds of rights. However, reifying civil rights and assuming they can have a meaningful existence without extensive social rights is to make citizenship vulnerable to dilution. The problem is that in liberal- ism civil rights and social rights are perceived as very different kinds of rights.

First, civil rights are seen as natural and as protecting the individual from interference. Because civil rights are seen as inalienable in the liberal tradition they are in a sense pre-political rights. Indeed the whole purpose of them is to protect the individual's basic liberties from the potentially damaging implications of political decisions, which may, for example, decide to abolish private property. Social rights, in contrast, are perceived as restrictions on economic freedom and as enhancing the power of the state. Second, social rights are seen as resource-dependent in a way that civil rights are not. This makes them vulnerable in times of economic recession. Third, for neo-liberals civil rights are inherently positive in their effects for they create autonomy and freedom. Social rights on the other hand can lead to a 'culture of dependency' and destroy the sense of personal innovation and initiative that are essential to the survival of the liberal state. All of these potential problems with social rights allowed the neo-liberal governments of the 1980s and 1990s in countries such as Britain and the USA to roll back social rights in the name of economic efficiency and the enhancement of people's civil freedoms. The problems that the capitalist system experienced from the 1970s onwards were blamed largely upon the growing expenditure on social rights and the associated growth of the bureaucratic and inefficient state that was strangling the freedoms of the market.

However, we should be cautious about accepting neo-liberal arguments at face value. Their claim to have reasserted people's civil rights – by cutting personal taxation, introducing market reforms into the public services, and by freeing up the labour market – is not sustainable. It is beyond the limits of this book to provide details of the various ways in which neo-liberal governments have failed to enhance citizenship. What is very clear however is that the kinds of rights asserted by neo-liberals are best termed market rights. By substituting this term for civil rights, we can get closer to understanding the dualism that liberals perceive exists between different types of right. Market rights, which first developed in the eighteenth century, are those rights necessary to the maintenance of a capitalist economy. The primary market right is therefore that of property. Market rights also include the right to accumulate and spend wealth as one sees fit, to assert self-interest in the market place, and to choose between a wide range of service providers. Crucially, market rights have often been asserted at the expense of civil rights as well as social rights. For example, up until the nineteenth century, trade unions were banned or suppressed in many liberal states. Other basic civil rights, such as protest and free speech, were ruthlessly opposed by the state in order to undermine any threats to the development of capitalism that might emerge. Similarly, during the neo-liberal experiment of the 1980s and 1990s, the marketisation of citizenship has been accompanied by growing police powers and restrictions on basic rights to free speech, association and protest. In Britain for example, between 1979 and 1997 the Thatcher and Major governments passed a series of laws that had a negative impact on civil citizenship (see Faulks 1998). The irony of neo-liberal government has been that despite their theoretical hostility to the state, in both Britain and America in particular the state has actually grown in its power. However, because of their scepticism concerning political rights, the democratic accountability of the state has lessened. In Britain, for example, many decisions that were previously taken by democratically elected bodies were transferred to unelected, government-appointed quangos. The main argument I am making here is that there is no necessary conflict between civil and social rights. Rather it is the assertion of market rights that prevents the fulfilment of the egalitarian elements of liberal citizenship. Without the material basis for citizenship that social rights provide, political rights are gravely undermined in their significance. What is more, attempts to weaken social rights have implications for civil rights as well.

The experience of neo-liberal government also exposes a further tension in liberal thinking about the differences between 'civil' and social rights. We have seen how social rights are perceived to be costly in a way that civil rights are not. But in reality, states spend far more of their income on defence and security, to safeguard civil rights, than they do on social expenditure. Raymond Plant (1992: 7, 21) makes a similar point when arguing that all rights require political planning and resources to be allocated to them. Civil rights are no more natural than social rights. Instead, the emphasis upon one at the expense of the other is ideologically determined. Moreover, the nature and content of all types of rights is forever contested. One only has to think of the example of gender here. It is only through the campaigns of feminists that many civil rights could be redefined in the interests of fairness and equality. For example, it is only since 1992 in Britain that men's 'sexual rights' over their wives to force women to have sexual intercourse against their will have been overturned. This means the question of what kinds of rights we should defend is a deeply political question; an argument that is directly opposed to the naturalistic assumption liberals make about civil citizenship.

Another legacy of the recent popularity of neo-liberalism, with its greater emphasis upon market rights, inequality and a coercive state, has been a growing division between active and passive citizens. This division has always existed, at least implicitly, within the liberal tradition. Partly this is due to liberalism's gendered assumptions, whereby men are seen as activists and women as the carers of men and children. The link between property and citizenship was also made clear in early liberal accounts of citizenship. Locke, for example, believed that it was property ownership that gave a person a stake in society, which is necessary for a commitment to a community's institutions and values. Owing to the liberals' neglect of the impact of social structures upon individual agency, they have also tended towards a harsh attitude to the poor. J. S. Mill, for example, defended the Victorian practice of workhouses because the poor required coercion rather than social rights to help them out of their predicament (Bellamy 1992: 30). The linkage of property to citizenship and the failure to acknowledge the complexity of power inequalities has been evident in neo-liberalism too. During the Thatcherite years in Britain, active citizens came to be seen as those who were able to assert their market rights of consumer choice, inequality and conspicuous consumption. Indeed, many of the Conservative government's policies enhanced the market rights of many. For example, the policy of selling council houses gave many people their opportunity to enter the property market. However, the commodification of citizenship also created greater divisions (Faulks 1998: 144–71). Material inequality grew sharply during the Thatcherite years. Moreover, those who could not take advantage of the new opportunities were increasingly labelled as 'work shy', or seen as part of a state-dependent 'underclass'.

Such language of exclusion was also closely linked to discourses of nationality. The social disorder that increased as a result of divisive policies was racialised by the government as they sought to blame, in the words of Margaret Thatcher, the influx of 'alien cultures' for the destruction of 'British' values (Faulks 1998: 164). The point that the neo-liberals failed to grasp was that without the necessary resources, people are often unable to exercise their rights. This means that when the Thatcherites extolled the virtues of active citizenship in a campaign in 1988, it was unlikely to meet with a positive response from those most in need of the benefits that the government was eroding. Women, the poor and ethnic minorities were most vulnerable to the dilution of their social rights and were more likely to lack the resources necessary to meet the government's demand that they take more responsibility for their own lives and for those of their family and local community.

This was also the case in other countries that fell under the sway of neo-liberalism. In an analysis of the attempt to cut Federal welfare budgets in the USA, O'Connor (1998) shows how the Reagan administration set out to discredit social rights. This was done by linking social citizenship to rising tax rates, which, it was alleged, were having a detrimental impact upon market rights. The Republicans also argued that it was welfare dependency, not poverty that was the root cause of America's inequalities. Links were also made between welfare benefits, gender and race. Welfare was seen as undermining the traditional family by encouraging illegitimacy and destroying the traditional male role as breadwinner. It also prevented, it was argued, ethnic minorities from exercising their market rights and climbing out of poverty. As O'Connor (ibid.: 55) puts it, like the Thatcherite governments in the UK, 'the White House utilized stereotypes and overgeneralizations to advance and sustain its own moralistic view of poverty'.

The dualisms I have identified thus far help to explain why liberals' emphasis is upon rights rather than responsibilities. The potential opposition liberals perceive between the interests of the individual and the needs of the wider community are reflected in their desire to keep the number and intensity of duties to a minimum. Of course, neo-liberal politicians have spoken about the need for responsibilities, but these are chiefly to assert one's market rights and to be self-reliant. The responsibilities asserted by neo-liberals have little to do with citizenship, since neo-liberals are suspicious of the kind of political activism that the responsibilities of citizenship entail. This privileging of rights in liberal thought has attracted substantial criticisms from those who place much greater emphasis on the responsibilities side of the citizenship equation. In the next section, I will explore some of these arguments. However, there are two dualisms in Figure 3.1 (page 57) still to mention. These are discussed in chapter 6, where I consider the implications of globalisation for citizenship. Briefly, however, both the tensions between sovereignty and human rights and between science and nature are becoming increasingly significant within the citizenship debate. First, globalisation is exposing the contradiction of liberalism's commitment to the exclusive state on one hand and equal rights on the other. Second, liberalism's support of rationalism, symbolised by scientific achievement, is becoming a threat to the most fundamental welfare right of all, namely the right to a healthy and sustainable ecology. This suggests that future conceptions of citizenship will need to give greater emphasis than does liberalism to the question of social responsibilities. This is true not just in relation to the environment. Liberalism has been justly criticised for its neglect of the duties and obligations of the citizen generally.

ARGUMENTS FOR CITIZENSHIP RESPONSIBILITIES

In recent years, there has been a sharp reaction against liberals' neglect of the responsibilities of citizenship. Social conservatives and communitarians in particular have argued strongly that an over-concentration on rights is detrimental to the quality of citizenship. Individual rights alone make for a thin and defensive form of citizenship that does little to maintain the political community upon which rights are founded. Daniel Bell (1976: 248–9) has identified a crisis in citizenship linked to what he sees as the contradictory processes of modern society:

> The economic dilemmas confronting Western societies derive from the fact that we have sought to combine bourgeois appetites which resist curbs on acquisitiveness, either morally or by taxation; a democratic polity which, increasingly and understandably, demands more and more social services as entitlements; and an individualist ethos which at best defends the idea of personal liberty, and at worst evades the necessary social responsibilities and social sacrifices which a communal society demands. In sum, we have no normative commitment to a public household or a public philosophy that would mediate private conflicts.

This passage captures well many of the concerns of critics of liberalism. The individualism of liberalism has encouraged a selfish and instrumentalist attitude to democracy and citizenship, which are not seen as expressions of communal life, but as methods for furthering self-interest. Rights are demanded, but no responsibilities accepted. Liberty has mutated into licence.

For social conservatives, the way to rejuvenate citizenship is to reconnect rights to responsibilities by making entitlements dependent upon the performance of duties. For example, Selbourne (1994: 61) contends that equal rights, without regard to desert or merit, are a 'false equality' that 'cannot serve the well-being of the civic order as a whole'. As in so many social conservative critiques, the main problem is seen as social rights. For Selbourne, the linkage between political and social rights has done much to destroy the sense of service associated with participation. Social rights create subjects, not citizens and have destroyed an ethic of civic virtue upon which the moral order is built. Moreover, state welfare is contingent in a way that political rights are not. Political rights are an expression of the popular sovereignty upon which the community is based and as such are inherent to the modern state. Social provision, on the other hand, should be firmly linked to desert and the performance of duty. For Mead (1986) this means that welfare should only be provided under strict conditions; Mead advocates a form of workfare, where social rights are dependent upon the recipient performing work that is guaranteed by the state. Both Himmelfarb (1995) and Etzioni (1995) also highlight the importance of social institutions, particularly the family, as sustaining the values necessary to social responsibilities. Etzioni (ibid.: 55) identifies the 'parenting deficit' as the crucial factor in explaining why young people in particular have failed to internalise a sense of obligation to society. The solution therefore is to legislate for moral behaviour and to pursue social policies that encourage marriage and discourage divorce.

All of these thinkers are to some extent correct to detect problems with the liberal emphasis upon rights. Because of liberals' assumptions about the relationship between the individual and the community, there has been a tendency to see responsibilities as an infringement of liberty, rather than a condition of autonomy. The naturalisation of rights also obscures the fact that all rights and responsibilities are made possible by the political community. There is the danger, therefore, that rights are asserted as absolutes, without considering their consequences for social order. To maintain our rights, we must be willing to accept the responsibilities that sustain the community. However, there are severe problems with the solutions offered by conservatives and communitarians.

There is a tendency amongst advocates of greater social responsibilities to adopt a cultural critique of modern society, and thereby to neglect the economic and political basis of citizenship. For example, the crisis of citizenship is attributed to a decline in morals. It is telling that Himmelfarb (1995) and Bell (1976) identify the 1960s as the key decade in explaining the development of a 'normless' society. The sexual revolution and culture of nihilism that developed in this decade has undermined the traditional values that had previously balanced the more acquisitive elements of human personality. Paradoxically this development of individual licence was accompanied by a creeping collectivism, as the welfare state took over many of the functions that had previously been undertaken by responsible citizens, through charity and the performance of good works. The problem here is that social conservatives identify some symptoms of the problems of liberal citizenship but treat them as the underlying cause. Like the liberals they criticise, they have a simplistic view of human agency and understate the role of power inequalities. The lack of a sense of obligation to society is therefore seen as a failing on the part of the individual, rather than an aspect of a wider social problem. Thus the institutions that are the real barriers to the performance of citizenship, principally the exclusive state and the inequalities of the market, are accepted uncritically. This means that in place of the liberals' assertion of an abstract individualism, many conservatives and communitarians assert an equally abstract vision of community. Such a misdiagnosis can only lead to policies that leave the roots of the problem untouched and create additional inequalities. The fact that many critics of liberalism advocate the reduction of rights, or at least a moratorium on the creation of new rights, is a threat to liberty, particularly for those vulnerable groups whose rights have still to be realised. Many of the 'solutions' offered by communitarians and conservatives risk negating some of the positive steps towards emancipation made by women for example. A return to traditional family structures risks recreating the division between women as carers and men as active citizens. It also risks stigmatising sexual minorities such as homosexuals whose civil rights are still far from certain, even in Western countries. Such policy prescriptions fly in the face of social changes that are unlikely to be reversed, and that have fundamentally changed the nature of gender relations and family structures.

To make social rights dependent upon work in the way that Mead suggests is also to ignore the fact that mass unemployment in Western societies since the 1980s is neither due to individual choice, nor a product of welfare benefits. Rather it is due to structural shifts in the nature of capitalism that have led to greater job insecurity. Labour markets in the USA and Britain in particular are characterised by an increase in part-time and temporary work, as well as long-term unemployment for many. The problem is that social rights, linked as they are to contributory systems through employment, are dependent upon the vagaries of market forces and as such provide an uncertain base for citizenship. To further stigmatise claimants by targeting or withdrawing benefits is not likely to lead to an enhanced sense of commitment to the community on behalf of the excluded. The neo-liberal revolution of the 1980s has shown that growing inequalities are hardly a basis for building citizenship and community. Indeed, the support of many conservative and communitarians for free market capitalism belies their alleged commitment to community. In reality, capitalism, with its emphasis upon short-term gain and the commodification of social relations, is unable to develop the kinds of obligations that conservatives and communitarians advocate.

Since communitarians accept the state uncritically, there is also the danger that an assertion of the needs of the 'community' may result in the promotion of the interests of the privileged majority in the name of the common good. It is also a mistake to attribute the problems of citizenship to 'too much democracy', as conservatives like Crozier (1975) have done. In fact, the reverse is true. The elitist structures of government that rights have depended upon have failed to develop the high level of political participation that is a defining characteristic of citizenship. One of the weaknesses of the social rights defended by Marshall (1992) was that they resulted largely from compromises between elites and were dependent upon a centralised and undemocratic state.

Are we left then with a choice between either a rights-based citizenship that fails to encourage responsibilities or an emphasis on responsibilities that undermines the rights of the vulnerable? The only way to move beyond this problem is to approach citizenship more holistically and to see rights and responsibilities not as intrinsically opposed, but as mutually supportive. This means exploring the content of citizenship in terms of the context in which rights and responsibilities are practised.

BEYOND FALSE DICHOTOMIES: THE NEED FOR HOLISTIC CITIZENSHIP

In this final section, I want to return to two of the fundamental tensions that liberals identify in citizenship. The first is that between rights and responsibilities. The second is between civil and social rights. In considering these problems, I will try to show why a holistic approach to citizenship is required.

Liberals are correct to identify the importance of rights to any rounded sense of citizenship. Rights are crucial to the successful resolution of the problems of governance, namely the need to distribute resources fairly and to maintain social order. The importance of rights is that they denote political agency and recognise the individual as worthy of respect and consideration. They are invaluable as a way of distributing resources according to the principles of justice and in the recognition of the equal status of each member of the community. Additionally, rights have an important role to play in sustaining social stability. Because of the diversity and creativity of humans, conflicts between them are inevitable. Often these conflicts are highly productive, and conflict certainly does not always involve violence. Indeed, the very purpose of politics, of which citizenship is a constituent part, is to resolve disputes through compromise. Rights play an important role in resolving social conflicts as they are a reminder that each individual is due the utmost respect and cannot be seen as a mere means to another's ends. Rights thereby offer some protection against the republican myth I discussed in chapter 2. The primary advocate of this myth is of course Rousseau, who, in his desire to unite the individual interests with that of the community, effectively advocated the annihilation of individual rights. Rousseau's infamous dictums such as the need to be 'forced to be free' or his advocacy of a civil religion to give the state a sacred mystique are methods for undermining the individual's autonomy. Surprisingly, given his republican credentials, many of the problems of Rousseau's theory of citizenship can be found in his distinctly liberal assumptions. Like Hobbes and Locke, he adopts the concept of the social contract to account for why a political community must be formed. However necessary this community might be, Rousseau believes that by giving up the liberties of the state of nature, individuals surrender their innocence as well. Thus, despite his republican pretensions, Rousseau believes that the community corrupts the individual. It is his mistrust of the individual's ability to shape his or her future democratically that leads him to advocate what amounts to an authoritarian state. His argument that the rules of a society must be determined by 'a superior intelligence' in the person of a lawgiver, for example, indicates Rousseau's reluctance to fully trust the democratic will (Rousseau 1968: 84).

Unfortunately, modern day republicans, who cite Rousseau as inspiration, also adopt his love of paradoxical terminology, which gives ammunition to liberal critiques who fear more responsibilities will come at the expense of individual freedom. For example, in defending a necessary distinction between citizens and strangers, Oldfield suggests that 'to remain a citizen one cannot always treat everyone as a human being'. Additionally, it may be necessary for the citizen to be 'shamed, disciplined and sometimes terrorised into living "civic virtue" as an expression of his authentic self' (Oldfield 1990: 8, 47). It is crucial to avoid such language if we are to reconcile the insights of liberalism and republicanism.

We must also avoid couching citizenship in pseudo-religious terms and theorising the state as an ethically superior entity. Despite the problems of Marx's theory of politics, his great contribution to citizenship theory has been to identify the material base of the state. This stands in contrast to the mystification of the state in writers such as Hegel, Green and Rousseau. The state is no symbol of the ethical life as Hegel believed but is a concrete institution that represents particular interests and bases its authority upon force. The importance of Marx's critique of liberal citizenship is that it begins to show why the rights of the liberal state represent a false universalism. As Thomas (1984) has rightly noted, one of Marx's main reasons for rejecting citizenship in its liberal form was that it was essentially a religious concept. In the liberal state citizenship becomes the new 'opium of the people'. Thomas uses the phrase 'alien politics' to describe the nature of a citizenship centred upon the exclusive state. He defines the modern state as 'the fake, ersatz universal, based not on the expression but on the alienation of people's communal capacities' (ibid.: 133). This is why communitarianism, without a critique of the state and the market conditions the state protects, amounts to little more than a wish-list of desirable behaviour. The failure of citizenship in liberal societies to generate appropriate obligations is not due to cultural or moral decline but rather to the political failures of the capitalist state. As Oldfield (1990) argues, too often in liberal theory civic virtue is seen as a threat to liberty, as the denial rather than the fulfilment of self. This is Marx's point too: alienation from oneself as a communal being results not from the performance of responsibility but from the exclusivity of the capitalist state.

While Marx wrote little on citizenship after completing *On the Jewish Question*, he assumed that in a communist society many of the positive values of citizenship, such as reciprocity and equality would be present. With the removal of private property and the withering away of the state, the bases for exploitation and alienation would be removed and the barriers to citizenship lifted. Marx borrowed the phrase 'from each according to his ability, to each according to his needs' to explain how a communist society would be one of cooperation, not competition between atomised individuals as in liberal society (Giddens 1994: 56). In the *Communist Manifesto* Marx identifies the interdependent nature of citizens when he argues that the free development of each is the condition for the free development of all. This contrasts with Marx's view of liberal rights, which he saw as encouraging individuals to see in others, not the fulfilment of but the limits to their freedom. Marx then provides a more sustainable communitarian view of citizenship than do present-day writers such as Etzioni. This is because he is willing to look beyond the appearance of citizenship to see how the context of a capitalist state destroys the meaning of citizenship as an expression of communal life. This is why Bernstein (1991: 110) considers Marx not to be opposed to rights as such but only to the limits liberal rights place on social and political participation:

> Marx's conclusion, which points to the overcoming of the duality between state and civil society, cannot be construed as recommending the overcoming of rights. On the contrary, the idea of individual man resuming the abstract citizen into himself points rather to individual man taking on in the world of civil society the attributes characterising the present political community . . . To extend the rights of the citizen to the whole of society is to see that rights are rights to participation in social life as a whole.

There is certainly an element of truth here. It is a plausible interpretation of Marx's early writings to argue that he saw that for political citizenship to have meaning, its influence must reach into civil society. However, we cannot overlook the fact that Marx, especially in his later works, did postulate his own version of the republican myth. By romanticising the proletariat as the vehicle to transform society from the vices of capitalism to the virtues of communism, he failed to see that any revolutionary act that utilised violence and sought to crush a section of society (the bourgeoisie) was doomed to failure. Marx's theory contains an anti-political (or authoritarian) aspect as he underestimates the transformative capacity of citizenship, relying instead upon the teleological forces of history. Marx is thereby guilty of under-emphasising political agency. He did not perceive that even in stateless communism the problems of governance, which citizenship seeks to resolve, would remain. A post-capitalist society could not therefore dispense with citizenship. The irony of actual communist regimes is that they have invariably had even more powerful states than those in liberal societies. The USSR may have had a constitutional commitment to rights but these were paternalistic and unconnected to any meaningful system of participation. Communist societies are more pre-liberal than post-liberal since they enshrine a version of subjecthood rather than democratic citizenship.

Nevertheless, Marx's critique of liberalism still provides us with significant insight into the false dualisms that liberalism assumes to be inherent to citizenship. This is not only the case with the relationship between rights and responsibilities. It is also true of the conflicts liberals see between different types of rights. As I have already said, there is no necessary conflict between civil and social rights. It is only if we accept liberal assumptions concerning the inevitability of the state and the primacy of the market over politics that certain kinds of civil freedoms appear to conflict with social citizenship. As I have argued, if we substitute the term market rights for civil rights we are more able to see the roots of this tension, which can be located in liberalism's suspicion of political interference with economic forces. The sanctity of market rights, however, rests upon several myths. The first is that such rights are natural and not political. This simply does not stand up to scrutiny. For Locke, natural rights were the gift of God. If we take the Supreme Being out of the equation, there is simply no reason to suppose that market rights are less dependent upon the sanction of the political community than are social rights. Second, the idea of the free market is itself illusory. No economy in history has operated outside of a political framework. Modern capitalism is no exception: its development was bound up with the creation of the nation-state. In many cases, such as in Japan and Germany, capitalism was largely created by the state. The question of the balance between economic and political priorities, then, is a question of degree. How many regulations we place upon the economic sphere is therefore a political question and, as I have already noted, civil rights require resources in the same way as do any rights. Third, liberals often defend the market on the grounds that it does not discriminate between individuals. Unlike political decisions, which consciously favour one interest over another, the market cannot produce injustices. However, the fact is that we can predict the outcomes of market interactions and can offset inequalities through social policy. Again, the question is not one of absolutes, but rather of balancing the utility of the market with maintaining the conditions for democratic citizenship.

The emphasis upon limited civil (or market) rights in liberal societies has shaped the way social citizenship has been defined and institutionalised. On this point, Frazer and Gordon have presented an interesting thesis. In an analysis of the apparent contradictions of civil and social rights in the USA, they point to how the dominance of civil citizenship has shaped the approach taken to social rights. The idea of contract, so central to the liberal tradition, has been applied inappropriately to social citizenship. Frazer and Gordon (1994: 91) believe that 'the result is a cultural tendency to focus on two, rather extreme, forms of human relationship: discrete contractual exchanges of equivalents, on the one hand, and unreciprocated, unilateral charity, on the other'. Both of these approaches are distorted expressions of social citizenship, as they assume a conflict between certain civil and social rights. As Frazer and Gordon (ibid.: 104–5) note, 'what is missing is a public language capable of expressing ideas that escape those dichotomous oppositions: especially the ideas of solidarity, non-contractual reciprocity, and interdependence that are central to any humane social citizenship'.

Fred Twine (1994) has taken up Frazer and Gordon's challenge by basing his defence of social rights on the fact that human beings are inherently social and interdependent creatures. Twine suggests that the atomistic vision of society that liberals present is an illusion because each individual's life course is intimately bound up with the lives of others. Individuals are interconnected in a number of ways. First, as political animals people can shape common institutions of governance only through collective deliberation. On this point Selbourne (1994) is right to argue that political rights are best understood not as ways to protect one's self-interest, but as a reflection of one's interconnectedness with the political community. Second, through the economic division of labour, individuals also find themselves dependent upon each other for the performance of services and the supply of goods. This means the production of wealth, and indeed the interactions of the market place, do not and cannot involve 'individuals as being involved in discrete and isolated market choice' (Twine 1994: 2). All market exchanges have external effects on others, as well as the buyer and seller. Such externalities have to be managed by the community collectively. This then dispels the liberal myth of atomised and rational consumers. Third, in our personal lives, we all find ourselves in a position of dependence at certain times in the life course. Sometimes we are carers and sometimes we are cared for. Finally, we exist in an interdependent relationship with nature that demands that we act responsibly towards the environment.

Twine's argument points to the need for a holistic approach to citizenship that recognises that citizenship does not just denote personal autonomy. It is also a status that recognises that our individuality is rooted in the community. As Dagger (1997: 15) has argued, autonomy and the performance of civic virtue are not necessarily at odds. The purpose of civic virtue, as understood in the ancient polis, was to avoid corruption and passive dependence upon the decisions of others. The performance of civic virtue is therefore an important safeguard of liberty and rights. As Selbourne (1994) contends, unless we address the lack of obligation individuals feel to the community, we run the risk of a more repressive moral order in the future. We cannot therefore reify one aspect of citizenship, as liberals do with market rights, or communitarians do with responsibilities, and expect citizenship to be effective. A holistic theory of citizenship that sees the interdependence between rights and responsibilities does not mean that we should make one dependent upon the other. To make rights dependent, for example, upon work would be to rob the individual of the opportunity to develop a sense of obligation to society: would removing the remaining stake that an individual has in society really compel them to good citizenship? No. Instead, we must work to remove the barriers to the performance of citizenship. Crucial here is recognising the material basis of citizenship and the direct relationship between the resources individuals possess and their willingness and opportunities to perform their rights and responsibilities. This does not of course prevent a society from requiring from its citizens a set of responsibilities. However, for responsibilities and rights to be seen as legitimate they must be linked to a more extensive participatory ethic than liberalism advocates and this ethic must be underpinned by extensive social rights (see chapter 5).

Questions about the content of citizenship and the balance between rights and duties are always contingent upon the decisions of community. This is why the notion of a social contract as the basis for citizenship is flawed. The idea of contract is too static. Instead, we need to accept that the requirements and aspirations of a community will change over time. Political participation is therefore central to uniting rights and responsibilities. It is through active campaigns against injustice that rights have been extended to previously excluded groups and the responsibility citizens have to promote justice within the community is exercised. The liberal approach to obligation, which tends to ask only that we obey the law, is too narrow a view of it. Obligation requires us to remain critical of our political institutions and to help those who are alienated from the system develop a sense of obligation and commitment to it. It is useful here to differentiate between different kinds of responsibilities. Duties may be seen as those responsibilities imposed by law and carry some kind of sanction if the individual does not honour them. Obligations, in contrast, may be seen as voluntary and as an expression of solidarity and empathy with others. The mark of a healthy society is its ability to rely upon obligations rather than imposed duties to maintain the conditions of the community. Where social conservatives like Selbourne (1994) have a point is that in liberal societies we are a long way from achieving the necessary level of social obligation. This means that for the foreseeable future we will have to accept more duties if we are to maintain the conditions of our citizenship rights (see chapter 5).

In this chapter, I have tried to show that the considerable strengths of liberal citizenship are undermined by its dualistic assumptions. A citizenship that is built upon the exclusive state and the inequalities of the market is a thin citizenship indeed. By emphasising the protection of market rights to the exclusion of responsibilities, liberals offer an unbalanced vision of citizenship. However, many critics make the mistake of simply reversing liberals' emphasis upon rights and argue for the dilution of rights and the assertion of duty. I have suggested that this is to miss the interdependent nature of rights and responsibilities, which must go together if the practice of citizenship is to be enriched. In chapter 5, I look at some ways in which the enhancement of citizenship might be achieved. In the next chapter, I continue my analysis of the content of citizenship by considering whether modernist perspectives of citizenship fail to address the needs of a pluralist and diverse society. Does social diversity demand a differentiated rather than universal citizenship?

4

PLURALISM AND DIFFERENCE

In the previous three chapters, we have seen that citizenship can
be exclusive as well as inclusive. The most obvious way that
citizenship operates as a privileged status is through the denial
of membership to non-nationals. While citizenship remains
closely tied to the nation-state, such exclusion is inevitable. I
will argue in chapter 6, however, that this relationship is becoming increasingly problematic as globalisation challenges the
boundaries of states. In this chapter, I wish to consider a different
form of exclusion that occurs within the borders of the state.
In its liberal form, citizenship claims to embody the ideal of
universalism. All individuals who can legitimately claim to be
citizens of the state are supposed to share equally the rights and
responsibilities of citizenship. For some critics, however, ironically it is this very claim to universality that acts as a powerful
exclusionary discourse. A notion of a universalised citizenship,
it is suggested, simply cannot be sustained in the context of
plural societies. In addition to individual rights, special group
rights are therefore required to ensure that some individuals are

not excluded from the benefits of citizenship because of their gender, 'race' or any other aspect of their identity. In this chapter, I examine this argument. The works of Iris Young and Will Kymlicka are generally acknowledged as powerful contributions to this debate. The chapter will therefore develop through a critical appraisal of their ideas. I will first outline Young's and Kymlicka's positions on citizenship, before developing a critique of their ideas in section two. In the final section, I analyse the relationship between equality and difference, which is central to understanding the problems generated by group rights. My guiding argument in this chapter is that group rights are incoherent and have negative implications for individual agency and for the practice of stable governance.

ARGUMENTS FOR GROUP RIGHTS

The essence of Young's (1989, 1990) case against liberal citizenship can be found in her analysis of the universality that it embodies. Young identifies three meanings of universality that are associated with liberalism. One of these she approves of, the other two are suspect. The first ideal of universality is that all members of a society are able to participate politically in the shaping of their lives. This is clearly a desirable end, and should be a goal for all democrats. Many of the barriers to this ideal concern the unequal distribution of resources such as money, time and information. However, the inequality of resources is only part of the problem. Even if we could overcome the material inequalities between citizens, the two other kinds of universality that liberalism entails would ensure, argues Young, that citizenship remains unequal in practice. This is because liberalism embraces a conception of citizenship that denies social differences. For Young (1989: 274), liberalism advocates not just universality in the sense of an equality of participation but also in the highly abstract sense of individuals adopting 'a universal point of view'.

Citizenship demands that individuals 'leave behind the perception they derive from their particular experience'. In short, citizens are required to deny their very identity when exercising their rights and responsibilities. The third meaning of universality is the practical implication of this. The laws that are made by citizens or their representatives apply to everyone, regardless of the diverse needs and inequalities that exist in society. Thus the structures of decision-making within liberal society prevent all voices from being heard effectively. Liberalism represents not equality between different individuals but the domination of the ideal of equality *over* difference: the diversity that characterises society is sacrificed in the name of an abstract and unattainable conception of citizenship.

Because individuals are not abstract rational creatures, but are products of cultural and social structures, they cannot, argues Young, achieve the kind of objective viewpoint that liberal citizenship demands. So any democratic institutions based upon such an abstract view of individuality must be faulty and unresponsive to people's needs. This by itself is a serious problem. In addition however, for Young, liberalism's approach to citizenship masks a set of unequal power relationships. These inequalities hide the fact that citizenship is defined in terms of, and therefore works in favour of, a particular social identity, namely that of white males. This bias is extremely deep-rooted and is historically bound up with imperialism and patriarchy. As was noted in the last chapter, citizenship has often been seen in the liberal tradition as for 'civilised' peoples only. Moreover, citizenship is theorised in liberalism in terms of objective reason and in opposition to emotion and the body. Thus women, who in the liberal tradition are the personifications of the irrational and emotional, are perceived as unable to fulfil the responsibilities of citizenship. Because of the deep roots of these inequalities, Young is correct to argue that they are often reproduced at an unconscious level. However, 'because moral theories tend to focus on deliberate action for which they seek means of justification, they usually do not bring unintended social sources of oppression under judgement' (Young 1990: 11).

To understand why citizenship serves to further the interests of some while excluding the needs of others we must, as Young insists, have a more developed theory of power than one that rests on individual intent. It is what I have called elsewhere the structures of power, such as the class system for example, which pervade liberal institutions and which result in material and cultural inequalities (Faulks 1999: 14–20). Young (1990: 39–65) discusses such structures of power through her development of a typology of oppression. She identifies 'five faces of oppression' which are: exploitation, marginalisation, powerlessness, cultural imperialism and violence. Any group that experiences one or more of these is the victim of oppression. By focusing upon individuals and ignoring the structural aspects of power, liberals tend to overlook or misunderstand how citizenship fails to serve all persons equally. This is true also of many republican thinkers who have as their ideal a civic unity enshrined in the status of citizenship. Young (1990: 117) contends that 'this ideal of the civic public . . . excludes women and other groups defined as different, because its rational and universal status derives only from its opposition to affectivity, particularity, and the body'.

To enhance citizenship we must take group identity seriously, for it is groups that 'constitute individuals' (Young 1990: 45). Moreover, social groups are so diverse that non-members of a particular group cannot fully understand the nature of that group's oppression. If citizenship is to be truly inclusive we must acknowledge the need for a politics of difference. By this, Young means that group identities must be incorporated into the decision-making institutions of the community. Young (1990: 184) summarises the policy implications of her proposal as follows:

I assert the following principle: a democratic public should provide mechanisms for the effective recognition and represen-tation of the distinct voices and perspectives of those of its constituent groups that are oppressed or disadvantaged. Such group representation implies institutional mechanisms and public resources supporting (1) self-organisation of group members so that they achieve collective empowerment and a reflective understanding of their collective experience and interests in the context of society; (2) group analysis and group generation of policy proposals in institutionalized contexts where decision makers are obliged to show that their deliberations have taken group perspectives into consideration; and (3) group veto power regarding specific policies that affect a group directly, such as reproductive rights policy for women, or land use policy for Indian reservations.

Young is keen to distinguish her theory of democratic citizenship from that of classical pluralists who see democracy as a compro-mise between predetermined positions represented by pressure groups. According to her definition, unlike in classical pluralism, social groups are determined not just by mutual interests but because their members share a particular way of life. Young's essentially cultural definition of the social group is reinforced by her argument that ideological groups do not count as social groups as she defines the term. Later in her argument, Young further narrows the definition of those social groups which are entitled to special rights. Young (1990: 187) asserts that 'specific representation' is only for 'oppressed or disadvantaged groups'. This principle, she argues, will prevent the proliferation of groups asserting their own case for rights.

In several ways, Young's theory of citizenship marks a break with the liberal tradition. The universalised notion of citizenship asserted by liberals, has, contends Young, led to the oppression of minorities and the denial of difference. It is only by asserting what she calls 'differentiated citizenship', built upon group rights, that pluralist societies can maintain order and move towards a just polity. In terms of the four dimensions of citizenship identified in chapter 1 (context, extent, content and depth), Young envisages a more extensive citizenship than liberals. The content of citizenship must emphasise group, rather than individual rights. The context of citizenship is not that of the homogenous community but a society that celebrates and protects difference rather than seeking to transcend it. Finally, it could be argued that Young's citizenship is thick rather than thin since it is rooted in the identities that constitute the individual, and as such is a more significant status than the narrowly public-orientated citizenship of liberalism.

Kymlicka (1995) attempts a somewhat different defence of group rights which, in contrast to Young, he maintains is more firmly rooted in the liberal tradition. However, like Young, Kymlicka also advocates a differentiated citizenship. He argues for what he calls 'multicultural citizenship' that recognises the importance of culture to an individual's sense of place and identity. Kymlicka notes that liberals have tended to see the relationship between the state and ethnicity as synonymous with that of the state and religion. According to this perspective, the best way to tackle the pluralist realities of modern society is to separate ethnic identity from the state in the same way that the church should be separated from the state. Particularistic identities should be confined to the private world. Citizenship should remain public, universal and culture-blind. The result of this approach has, however, been 'to render cultural minorities vulnerable to significant injustice at the hands of the majority, and to exacerbate ethnocultural conflict' (Kymlicka 1995: 5). The traditional liberal defence of natural rights cannot solve the problems of differences within the state. Therefore Kymlicka (1995: 6) advances a theory of minority rights: 'A comprehensive theory of justice in a multicultural state will include both universal rights, assigned to individuals regardless of their group membership, and certain group-differentiated rights or "special status" for minority cultures.'

It is important to note that Kymlicka uses the term culture interchangeably with the term 'nation' and 'a people'. He has in mind then ethnic groups, rather than groups based on say, class or gender. However, he is careful to argue that the national groups he discusses are not defined in terms of 'race' or descent (Kymlicka 1995: 22). The importance of ethnic identity is that it provides the cultural context in which individuals develop and therefore sets the parameters for individual choice. For Kymlicka (1995: 83), 'the availability of meaningful options depends on access to a societal culture, and on understanding the history and language of that culture'. Given the importance of the context national culture provides for citizenship, Kymlicka considers it essential that the polity supports all those ethnic cultures that its members consider important. To this end, Kymlicka envisages three kinds of group rights.

First, self-government rights involve the devolution of powers to minorities within the state. This is likely to lead to some form of federal polity. Second, there are polyethnic rights, which protect group identity through legal and public financing of minority cultures. Third are special representation rights that give guaranteed representation for minorities in the community's political institutions. Self-government rights are obviously more extensive and are one step away from secession. Polyethnic and representation rights, however, more clearly involve the integration of minorities into the polity; not through the denial of cultural differences but rather through the recognition of those differences as an essential part of a stable multicultural state.

Such an accommodation of difference acknowledges that liberal citizenship is traditionally defined 'by and for white, able-bodied, Christian men', and recognises that citizenship is an inherently 'group-differentiated notion' (Kymlicka 1995: 124, 181). In a world where citizenship is determined by the state, decisions about who is entitled to the status are based on an individual's group membership. It is Kymlicka's contention that we should apply this same principle to groups within states and seek to accommodate their needs accordingly. Although their arguments differ, Young and Kymlicka both arrive at the conclusion that citizenship must be rooted in a notion of the social group. Citizenship cannot be purely an individual status because citizenship only has meaning to the individual in the wider cultural context of the group.

AGAINST A POLITICS OF DIFFERENCE

Young and Kymlicka undoubtedly raise important and difficult questions concerning the universality of citizenship. Both are correct to identify how liberal theories of citizenship have tended towards highly abstract conceptions that deny the social character of the individual. A disembodied and atomistic definition of the citizen ignores the barriers that exist to the exercise of rights and responsibilities. In focusing their attention upon the experience of minorities or, in the case of Young, oppressed groups in general, both authors begin to identify how the inequalities inherent in liberal society negate the promise of meaningful equality. If the important question of the context of citizenship is not addressed, the danger that universality can crush social difference does indeed exist. Vulnerable groups are at risk of having their needs ignored and their voices left unheard. Both Young and Kymlicka meet the challenge of inequality by advocating a change in the content of citizenship to include group-differentiated rights alongside individual rights. They avoid the temptation to reject entirely the emancipatory potential of citizenship. Such a rejection is often explicitly made in postmodern accounts of social life which, while often insightfully deconstructing the assumptions that lie behind many apparently neutral concepts such as citizenship, fail to advance the alternative conceptual tools that are necessary to deal with the inherent human problem of governance. A more constructive postmodern approach is to build upon the strengths of liberalism and to make its promises real by identifying and overcoming the barriers to their fulfilment. The theories of Young and Kymlicka must then be welcomed as valiant attempts to overcome the problems of modernity. I wish to argue however that the arguments for group rights are incoherent and are therefore unlikely to enhance citizenship.

The first problem with a citizenship centred upon groups is ascertaining what groups can legitimately claim to be special cases and are therefore deserving of additional entitlements not available to other members of a polity. Young's definition of groups as being constituted by those who share a particular way of life is unsustainable. In seeking to transcend what Young sees as the essentialist individualism of liberal citizenship, she merely replaces it with an equally essentialist definition of the social group. Young quite rightly wishes to argue against defining individuals in static terms, which denies them the capacity to grow and to change. But in identifying women, for example, as necessarily having a shared experience and thereby classifying them as a social group is to commit the very error that Young accuses liberals of. To deny the internal differences that exist within the various social groups she sees as being oppressed is to overlook the fact that every individual has multiple identities and social roles. All of these identities may be equally important to the individual. To ask an individual to base their political position on a single fragment of their identity is therefore a denial of their complex individuality. Moreover, one aspect of an individual's identity might be tension with another: one's identity as a black woman could at certain moments be in tension with one's identity as a member of the working class and so on.

If we are to have a citizenship that fully acknowledges individual agency, and in particular the capacity for self-governance, we cannot define individuals in terms of any single part of their identity. A theory of citizenship based upon group rights risks freezing social differences and creating an uncommunicative, fragmented and highly static politics. This is hardly likely to lead to the transcendence of oppression that Young seeks.

Another problem with Young's formulations is this: what is to prevent a proliferation of new groups demanding rights and thereby fragmenting the polity still further? Young's answer can be found in her discussion of the five faces of oppression (see p. 86), which she considers to be 'objective criteria' for ascertaining the legitimacy of rights claims. What makes a group's claim legitimate is that it is subject to one or more of these five aspects of oppression. Young's definition of oppression, however, is clearly far from objective, is contradictory, and therefore unhelpful in identifying the forms of oppression particular social groups experience. Her wish to differentiate between forms of oppression leads Young to some bizarre conclusions. She states that 'working-class people are exploited and powerless but if employed and white do not experience marginalization and violence' (Young 1990: 64). This conclusion is so clearly unsustainable that it requires little comment. Does a working-class person who works in a tedious, insecure, unsafe manual job and who lives on a run-down, crime-ridden council estate not experience marginalisation and violence? In addition, the bases of oppression change, as do the ways that individuals identify their interests. In recent years people of mixed parentage in the USA have been arguing strongly to be classified as a group worthy of special treatment. Tellingly, this has been opposed by many ethnic leaders. What this illustrates is the largely arbitrary nature of awarding rights according to group membership. It also shows the potential tension that exists between groups competing for special status. Joppke (1998) has argued that in fact many of the official 'victim' categories in the USA, such as Asian or Hispanic, are extremely artificial constructs. Moreover, the strategy of multicultural citizenship has other dangers. For instance, in the context of calls for greater multiculturalism in France, 'the new racism of Le Pen emulates the multicultural right to be different' (Joppke, 1998: 38). In other words, the politics of group identity can play into the hands of the powerful.

Oppression, then, is a more complex problem than Young acknowledges. Crucially, oppression is relational in character. As Hegel's famous discussion of the master–slave relationship illustrates, the oppressor is also enchained by his or her oppression (Williams 1997). This is also Marx's point when he argues that capitalism is alienating for the capitalist as well as for the worker. We must seek to free the oppressor as well as the oppressed if we are to be rid of relationships based upon domination. To overcome the damaging effects of oppression we must look to develop trust between groups and not just *within* groups. When rights and obligations are working well, they build empathy between very different individuals who nevertheless share many common experiences and have a mutual interest in maintaining the basis for communal life. However, Young builds her defence of group rights on the idea that only those who experience oppression (as defined by Young) can understand that oppression. Only those who are oppressed are truly authentic and can claim special rights. Anne Phillips (1993: 84), despite developing a strong critique of Young's ideas herself, defends Young on the grounds that Young wishes a polity where 'we acknowledge others as being of equal account'. However, this is just what Young effectively denies in her emphasis upon oppression as an experience that cannot be understood except by the oppressed. This has serious implications for Young's approach to democracy.

Given the discredited status of classical pluralist theory, Young is keen to distance herself from it. However, as McLennan (1995: 96–7) notes, Young is unsuccessful in differentiating her theory from the pluralism of writers such as Dahl (1961). This is largely because, like the pluralists she criticises, the social groups she identifies arrive at the democratic assembly with their minds already largely made up. Their status as oppressed groups give their arguments a moral force and an understanding of power that groups representing white males lack. It is implicit in her argument, therefore, that some voices are more authoritative than others. Moreover, in her defence of veto powers, Young effectively removes some crucial issues from the political agenda. For example, she argues that women have the sole right to reproductive rights. However, the only logical reason for defending this position is because of women's biological differences from men. Given Young's critique of essentialism, this marks an important contradiction in her argument for it seeks to base rights claims on predetermined, naturalistic criteria.

To deny that one group can understand the experiences of another has very dangerous implications for the quality of deliberation: it sets the limits of democracy before a word has been spoken. If, for example, men can never understand women's oppression, what incentive is there to encourage men to develop empathy and to adopt a critical stance towards their own behaviour? As John Hoffman (1995: 209) remarks, 'no one can understand themselves unless they are also able to understand others'. It is particularly crucial for those who suffer most from domination to transform the way that others see that oppression. To deny the capacity to empathise with the plight of others is to allow oppression to continue. Politics then becomes little more than a method through which group difference is affirmed (Miller 1995: 132). For this reason, Young's essentialist theory is unlikely to lead to a deliberative democracy. As Miller (1995a: 446) argues, Young fails to identify how or why diverse groups will be reconciled. She appears to assume, observes Miller, that 'when the groups she identifies as oppressed make their case, this case will overwhelm the opposition'.

Young's naivety in these matters is compounded by her romanticised view of social groups. As Phillips (1993: 160) argues, 'the oppressed have no monopoly on good behaviour, being a victim is not a guarantee of right'. The response of oppressed groups to their situation can be negative as well as positive. Historically it has resulted in separatist movements, which turn discrimination on its head, terrorism and calls for vengeance, as well as more constructive alternatives. In addition, to judge individuals by their group membership is to risk violating those individuals' freedom. This problem is inherent in all collective identities. An obvious example of how an individual can suffer from his or her group membership is that of hostage-taking for political reasons. Thus the British hostage John McCarthy, who was held captive by Islamic fundamentalists in the Middle East for several years, was apparently told when captured that this was not his problem, but 'his country's problem'. By inviting others to treat us as members of a particular group we risk creating a tension between individual rights and this collective identity. One of the most important reasons to have rights is precisely to protect the individual from such arbitrary treatment. A citizenship based upon groups rather than individuals may well lead then to more, not less oppression. We must also remember that groups can themselves be oppressive of their members. This brings me to the problem of the reification of culture, a consideration of which throws light upon Kymlicka's as well as Young's theories of differentiated citizenship.

Like Young, the basis for group rights in Kymlicka's theory is cultural. However, the shared way of life that Kymlicka identifies as constituting a group worthy of special rights is not determined by oppression, as such, but by national identity. Crucially, to justify his theory, Kymlicka makes what he calls an analogy to states. His logic is as follows. States are the pre-eminent political organisations in the world. It is nation-states that therefore define who is a citizen and who is not. Consequently, citizenship is an inherently group-orientated idea since it is linked to the membership of a culturally defined collectivity. This means that, logically, we cannot deny group rights to national groups that do not enjoy statehood. However, just as Young's acknowledgement of the multifaceted and overlapping nature of social identities is in tension with her defence of clearly defined groups for the purposes of determining special rights, so Kymlicka's theory too falters on his definition of culture. The problem is that while rights are comparatively concrete things in that they bestow certain material benefits, culture is clearly fluid and ever changing. Indeed, it could be argued that a culture that is unchanging is a dead culture. Any notion of culture, whether it rests on a shared sense of oppression or a national identity seems then a highly unstable basis for citizenship rights.

In basing his theory of citizenship on national culture Kymlicka runs into the same problems that we identified in Miller's theory of nationality in chapter 2. He assumes that choices that citizens make are meaningful only in the context of the nation. Kymlicka (1995: 69) asserts that 'individual freedom is tied to membership in one's national group'. But why must we accept this? As I argued in chapter 2, the concept of national culture hides many divisions such as class and gender. What is more, national discourses are often used by elites to gloss over these differences and excuse them from tackling the roots of inequalities. Kymlicka, in linking meaningful choices to national culture, also runs into the problem of distinguishing between meaningful and meaningless choices (Fierlbeck 1998). It may be that the identities that an individual most values are not their ethnicity or nationality but the ideological or lifestyle choices they make. Kymlicka appears to favour national identity above other sources of meaning because of its basis in history. Yet, as we have seen, historical nationality has had an ambiguous relationship to citizenship. The reality is that often a defence of one's national identity is made and sustained in opposition to another's sense of identity. Thus in Northern Ireland, for instance, the very essence of many Unionists' sense of national identity is to be found in their anti-Catholicism and hostility to the civil rights claims of Catholics living in the North. National identity cannot be so easily detached from religion, sectarianism, and ethnic hostility as Kymlicka seems to suggest. Kymlicka (1990: 172) writes that 'the primary good . . . is the cultural community as a context of choice, not the character of community or its traditional ways of life'. However, national characteristics and the values so dear to many nationalities often stand in tension with citizenship's emphasis upon human agency. It is essential to the practice of citizenship that we remain critical of the received wisdom of the past if we are to overcome the divisions that strong attachments to the nation often entail. Thus, the nature of a particular culture *is* crucial. This leads us into highly controversial territory, for how do we reconcile illiberal practices with liberal ideals of individual freedom? Kymlicka attempts to tackle this problem by advocating a distinction between internal and external cultural restrictions. Liberals should, he argues, defend group rights because they recognise the reality of cultural differences and promote diversity as a social good by protecting minority cultures from the majority. However, liberals should argue against internal restrictions that infringe the civil rights of members of a cultural group. This clearly stands in tension with Kymlicka's argument that what matters is not the nature of a culture as such, but rather the necessary context *any* culture, however oppressive, provides for the choices we make as citizens. Like Young, his theory is compromised by his reliance on a predetermined cultural identity as a basis for citizenship.

Young and Kymlicka identify some real problems with liberal citizenship. They are right to worry about the implications for citizenship that the neglect of important social differences entails. It is tempting to seek to defend vulnerable minorities through the development of group rights. However, there is no non-arbitrary way of determining which groups deserve such special provision. Young and Kymlicka assert a particularistic and essentialist definition of culture which amounts to a denial of the human agency that citizenship must recognise if it is to be truly inclusive. As Fierlbeck (1998: 99) contends, 'to assert that one simply knows that another person is defined predominately by their culture or specific group traits rather than other factors seems as oppressive as refusing to believe that cultural characteristics are important at all'. Young's argument for group rights, based as it is upon a shared sense of oppression, is likely to meet with increased hostility to minorities, as well as leading to the further fragmentation of society. By uncritically embracing the state as the only plausible polity and linking this to a national culture, Kymlicka unwittingly advocates conditions that can only exacerbate the tensions between majorities and minorities. Indeed Kymlicka (1995: 9, 108) acknowledges that 'the state unavoidably promotes certain cultural identities, and thereby disadvantages others'. He is also aware that globalisation has 'made the myth of a culturally homogenous state even more unrealistic'. He is, however, unwilling to develop the logic of such comments into a post-statist theory of citizenship. Kymlicka's defence of state sovereignty serves only to highlight further the contradictions at the heart of liberal citizenship between equal rights and national sovereignty.

CITIZENSHIP, EQUALITY AND DIFFERENCE

In the final section of this chapter, I shall explore in a little more detail some of the problems for a universal citizenship raised by group rights. In particular, I shall consider the relationship between equality and difference, which seems to be the most crucial issue raised by theories of differentiated citizenship. This discussion will, I hope, lead naturally to a consideration of how citizenship can be enhanced, which is the subject matter of the following chapter.

As Pateman (1992) observes, the problematic relationship between equality and difference has bedevilled much feminist analysis of citizenship in particular. Women have often appeared to be faced with the choice of whether to argue for incorporation into an inherently masculine conception of citizenship, an incorporation that can only be achieved by denying their differences from men, or whether to assert a politics of difference, which jettisons ideas of universal citizenship and argues instead for special rights and responsibilities. However, there is no reason to suppose that equality and difference are inherently in opposition. In chapter 3 I discussed how the dominant liberal perspective of citizenship could be understood in terms of its dualistic logic. Because of the assumptions liberals make about the relationship between the individual and community, and in their eagerness to preserve a market-dominated private sphere, liberal citizenship is abstract in form. The opposition between equality and difference can be seen as a product of this abstract individualism. Equality and difference is another false dichotomy that we must seek to dissolve. Pateman shows in fact how early campaigners for women's citizenship such as Mary Wollstonecraft argued for equal rights *and* for their differences with men to be acknowledged. The only way this can begin to be achieved is through adopting a relational rather than atomistic theory of citizenship. As Pateman rightly holds, the choice between equality and difference is a false one. The main barrier that prevents the development of a relational citizenship, which sees equality and difference as complementary, is that of domination.

Young's emphasis upon oppression and her advocacy of group rights are clearly attempts to problematise domination and move beyond it. As I have argued, however, Young's approach to domination is not a relational one. She doubts that the oppressors can understand their own natures and thereby empathise with the oppressed. Implicitly, then, Young takes up a position on the question of equality and difference which favours an assertion of the latter over the former. Kenan Malik has eloquently pointed to the problems with such a strategy. Malik argues that equality must remain the essential goal for radicals if emancipation is to be achieved and citizenship is to be inclusive of diverse identities. In classical liberalism, Malik observes, equality was naturalised and rights granted by God. Marx however more persuasively rooted equality firmly in social relations. The main point for Malik (1996: 258) is that 'once essential explanations, whether natural or social, are excluded, the very idea of equality also becomes subordinate to the "contingency of prevailing identities"'. So, the danger of a politics of difference is that the assertion of diversity becomes the very rationale for politics. Of course, politics presupposes difference. Without diversity and conflicts of interests, we would have no need for politics. However, the whole point of politics is to look for areas of compromise, to build common interests and to create systems of governance that are able to accommodate differences peacefully. To place too much stress upon difference and to deny the ability of humans to understand each other's position is to reject implicitly the possibility of equality. Citizenship as a shared project that involves diverse, but intrinsically social, individuals building common institutions that sustain their lives becomes impossible. The general perspective on social issues that Young rejects as unrealisable is in fact just what citizenship requires us to develop. It is only by looking beyond our own experiences that we can deliberate effectively and can thereby hope to maintain social order. Malik (ibid.: 265) is in no doubt that a politics of difference cannot achieve the emancipation of excluded groups:

> The philosophy of difference is the politics of defeat, born out of defeat. It is the product of disillusionment with the possibilities

of social change and the acceptance of the inevitability of an unequal, fragmented world . . . The consequence has been the celebration of marginality, of parochialism and indeed of oppression. Transcending such an outlook requires not simply intellectual conviction but political aspiration.

However, such political aspiration towards equality need not deny difference. As Young (1990: 98) herself observes, difference need not mean 'a complete absence of relationship or shared attributes'. Logically, an aspiration towards equality presupposes difference. The aim of equality is precisely to recognise and protect diversity by respecting the rights of all individuals, regardless of their beliefs or identity. This is why it is potentially dangerous to base an individual's citizenship on any single aspect of their identity or membership. Kymlicka's position on this question is particularly revealing because, while Young is explicitly critical of the whole liberal tradition, Kymlicka seeks to justify his theory according to liberal values. By tackling the difficult questions of equality and difference in liberal terms Kymlicka unwittingly reveals the real source of the problem, namely the state.

Again we come back to Kymlicka's definition of citizenship as an inherently group-based concept. It is because Kymlicka defines citizenship in this way that he is able to argue that individual rights are complemented and not jeopardised by the addition of group rights for some minorities. However, Kymlicka mistakes expediency for principle. Citizenship is only defined culturally because of the existence of the state which determines social membership by nationality. As Fierlbeck (1998: 102) cuttingly puts it, much of Kymlicka's argument is based on the strategy of 'if it exists, then it must be logically coherent'! However, as I argued in chapter 1, classical liberals were highly suspicious of the state. Kymlicka, in contrast, makes a virtue of the state by arguing that one of its essential functions is to preserve cultural difference. Yet elsewhere Kymlicka (1995: 83) contends that 'cultures do not have fixed centres or precise boundaries'. The result of this contradiction is that by linking rights to ethnic groups, we ground citizenship on constantly shifting foundations. As Waldron (1992: 781–2) reasons, humans undoubtedly need some cultural context, but why should we assume, as the logic of Kymlicka's theory implies, that 'the social world divides up neatly into particular distinct cultures'? It is because Kymlicka is so attached to the state that he fails to see that an alternative and more fruitful path to justice would be to ensure that individual rights are not violated by states. This, of course, would require a basic rethinking of the nature of political community and would inevitably require the development of institutions of global governance beyond the state. It is this position that is consistent with liberalism, however, not the group-based model of citizenship that Kymlicka advocates.

Kymlicka is right to argue that human rights discourses have so far failed to tackle the problem of minority cultures, but this is precisely because the state that Kymlicka defends prevents human rights from being applied equally. Moreover, minority cultures can be as oppressive of their members' needs as majorities can be of minorities. To argue that one's individual freedom is tied to membership in the national group creates multiple problems for all individuals who are oppressed by the dictates of their 'community leaders'. This is particularly a problem for women, who have often found that a defence of cultural practices means condoning such acts as female circumcision or the forced abduction and rape of young girls as a legitimate method of acquiring a wife, a practice that occurs in parts of Southern Ethiopia. This is why during South Africa's transition to democracy, women's groups fought so hard to have civil rights embedded in the constitution, so as to override tradition and customs that have often involved discriminatory practices against women (Yuval-Davis 1997: 78).

As Kymlicka himself observes, many cultures are illiberal and present considerable problems for individual liberty. However, once we accept the logic that groups can have rights there is no reason to prevent new groups, potentially undesirable in their beliefs, claiming such rights. Kymlicka does attempt to address aspects of this problem. He believes that immigrants to liberal states, because they have entered voluntarily, are in no position to demand rights to self-government. However, this is a very naive view of the reasons why migration occurs. The push and pull factors of migration very often involve poverty, political persecution, religious discrimination, and so on. A purely voluntaristic theory of immigration is hardly realistic. This reveals Kymlicka's failure to address the problem of how the states system and its promotion of neo-liberal market reforms has undermined the rights of many across the developing world and has intensified migratory flows. Kymlicka argues that group rights are essential to a fair society. He also contends that the expedient rejection of such rights by political elites often sacrifices justice for stability. Logically then, Kymlicka cannot sustain an objection to involuntary immigrants demanding group rights where they have been the victims of state injustice. Kymlicka (1995: 224) does in fact accept that unjust acts by the state do alter the legitimacy of rights claims when he writes that 'a country forfeits its right to restrict immigration if it has failed to live up to its obligations to share its wealth with the poorer countries'. Having conceded this, however, it is difficult to see how immigrants cannot justly demand special rights given the fact that the majority of Western governments clearly have not fulfilled their obligations to the global community. This problem is even more acute if we consider groups who are acknowledged as ethnic groups, worthy of self-government rights, but who clearly have not arrived voluntarily. Consider for example the black group, the Nation of Islam, in the USA. At various times in its history this movement has advanced a separatist and overtly racist, particularly anti-Semitic, position. And yet, as an ethnic group that has arrived largely in America as the result of slavery, any claim they might make for self-government rights is hard to resist if we accept Kymlicka's (1995: 126) position that group rights represent compensation for past injustices. Elsewhere Kymlicka slides from his defence of group rights based on justice, to a denial of rights in the name of stability. In considering the United Nations' defence of 'self-determination' of peoples, he (1995: 117) argues that to put this principle into practice would be 'destabilising'. But if we assign agency to groups in the way that Kymlicka suggests, then there is no principled reason to prevent any group that defines itself as a nation from forming its own polity if it so wishes.

A consideration of the relationship between equality and difference shows, then, that group-differentiated citizenship presents major problems for building the kind of communicative politics necessary to constitute equality and to preserve diversity. In Young's theory, group rights risk freezing individuals into fragmented groups that can only ever represent part of any individual's identity, and offer little hope for developing a common citizenship that aims not at *homogeneity* but *solidarity*. The national groups that Kymlicka makes central to his theory of citizenship can also be oppressive of individual rights, for such identities often privilege cultural unity over individual choice. Despite Kymlicka's valiant attempt to defend group rights from a liberal perspective, it seems to be that group rights are inherently opposed to the individual rights advanced by liberalism. We should not make the mistake of assuming that because the ideas of liberalism are undermined by the context in which they operate, we must therefore reject these values altogether. The key to understanding why the liberal promises of security, autonomy and equality are not fulfilled is to be found in the liberal assumptions of the inevitability of the nation-state, and in their assertion of the superiority of the market over

democracy in allocating the resources necessary to the practice
of citizenship. These problems are further investigated in the
next two chapters.

5

ENHANCING CITIZENSHIP

Undoubtedly citizenship has great potential as an idea that challenges injustices within and across societies. It was liberalism that began to extend the reach of citizenship through its defence of equality and individual rights. These liberal ideals moved citizenship beyond the exclusive connotation citizenship had in the pre-modern world. However, radicals are right to want to reconstruct the idea of citizenship in ways that transcend the limits of liberalism. This means building upon the foundations of liberalism, rather than seeking a completely new basis for citizenship. The challenge is to look for ways in which the promise of liberal citizenship can be fulfilled. In this chapter, I shall sketch out some proposals for how this might be achieved.

First, I consider the context of citizenship. In particular, I am interested in the relationship between citizenship and the political community. I will contend that citizenship is closely related to democracy. It is an ethic of participation, which only democratic systems of governance encourage, that is the key to uniting rights and responsibilities. Since the basis of our individual rights is the political community, we must be willing to accept a greater responsibility for its maintenance. However, to increase responsibilities without addressing the barriers to their fulfilment would only lead to greater social inequality. Enhancing the content of citizenship means addressing rights and responsibilities as reciprocal ideas. In section two, therefore, I make the case for a citizens' income, which seems to me to be the key to reconstructing social rights in a way that decommodifies citizenship. Finally, I shall explore how citizenship might be intensified by the idea of 'intimate citizenship'. This concept implies that the rights and responsibilities of citizenship have a role to play in our personal as well as our public lives.

CITIZENSHIP AND POLITICAL COMMUNITY

Citizenship is a status that mediates the relationship between the individual and the political community. Citizenship also provides a framework for the interactions between individuals within civil society. The advantage citizenship has over other social identities is that it has an inclusive quality that other identities such as class, religion or ethnicity lack. The recent popularity of citizenship amongst radicals can in part be explained by the widespread realisation that social struggles based upon exclusive identities have an inherently authoritarian character. For example, as Phillips (1993) argues, there is a tendency amongst Marxists to see social differences as a distraction to the primary conflict between classes. It follows from this that identities other than class must be suppressed if communism is to be achieved. The dangers of such group exclusivity, whether it is based upon class or ethnicity, is the main reason why I argued against the notion of group rights in chapter 4. It is hazardous to attribute positive or negative characteristics to individuals on the basis of their membership of a social group. We must instead build upon liberals' emphasis upon citizenship as an individual status.

The relationships between the polity and its citizens, as well as between citizens themselves, are reciprocal and interdependent however, even if this is not always recognised by the individuals involved. This means that rights and responsibilities of citizenship are logically closely related. Rights imply responsibilities, since rights do not exist in a vacuum. To be effective, others must recognise and respect our rights and we have a responsibility to do the same. Rights also depend for their existence on the maintenance of the political community that sustains them. Consequently, we have a responsibility to exercise our rights, where these rights are fundamental to the good of the community. A healthy polity, then, needs an active citizenry. Active citizenship begins with the individual, since it is through individual actions that the structural conditions of citizenship are reproduced and improved. Political reform must therefore look to improve the opportunities for citizens to exercise their rights and responsibilities by promoting an ethic of participation. It is only by actively exercising citizenship that the false opposition between rights and responsibilities can be dissolved. Reform must also aim at increasing awareness of the relational nature of individuality. One of the most damaging effects of an emphasis upon natural rights in liberalism has been to encourage atomism and instrumentalist attitudes towards our rights. This is where communitarian critics of liberalism have a point. If we believe that our rights are unrelated to the communities in which we live then we will endanger the very existence of our entitlements.

One of the purposes of citizens' responsibilities is to strengthen the ties that bind individuals together and to thereby offset the atomistic tendencies of liberalism. In liberal societies today, the opportunity structures for the exercise of citizenship are clearly failing to do this. Studies of political participation show a worrying decline in the faith citizens have in their political systems and in their representatives (Dalton 1996). Voting turnouts have fallen in most Western countries in the last few years and many political parties have experienced declining membership. This at a time when mass higher education and the enormous increase in the influence and range of information media have enhanced citizens' general political awareness. Since the Second World War, many societies have also witnessed a consistent increase in instances of anti-social behaviour, with crime being an obvious example. Such behaviour can be explained in part by the alienation people feel towards their communities. These problems go a long way towards explaining the growing significance of the communitarian movement (Tam 1998). Communitarians have stressed the need for society to demand greater responsibilities from its citizens as a corrective to the entitlement revolution that since 1945 has undermined the legitimacy of the state, which, communitarians argue, cannot hope to meet the ever-increasing demands of its people.

Communitarians are right to stress the need for a greater sense of citizen responsibility. However, this cannot happen at the expense of rights. Neither can we attribute society's problems to the cultural sphere, as many communitarians have been tempted to do. The kinds of development that Etzioni and others identify as negative, such as the sexual liberation of the 1960s and changes in family structures, reflect the struggles for equal citizenship by women and sexual minorities. As Turner (1994: 166) has argued, the apparent postmodern cultural conditions in which we now live can be interpreted as the logical consequence of liberalism, with its stress upon individuality and equality. Indeed, the values of liberalism have facilitated the most diverse and pluralistic communities in history. We cannot, and should not, resist the positive and egalitarian social changes that have taken place in many post-war societies in the areas of sexuality, gender politics, music and art. In the context of late modern social conditions a return to tradition is no longer possible.

Beck (1997: 95) detects a process in Western society which he calls individualisation. The breakdown or decline of traditional reference points such as religion, class, nation or stable employment mean that individuals 'must produce, stage and cobble together their biographies themselves'. One interpretation of individualisation is that advanced by those who advocate a 'politics of difference'. Extreme individualism could lead us to the conclusion that the many different interests within society are simply too diverse to be reconciled through a universal citizenship. However, as was argued in the previous chapter, the irony is that writers who subscribe to such a view have often tended to advocate group identity as the main agent of politics, and as such deny the very individuality they claim to defend. Nevertheless, the fragmentation of an increasingly individualised society must be tackled in some way. If political community is to be sustained, citizenship must play an important role in the reconstruction of identity in an ever more individualistic age.

The ties that bind the community together cannot be cultural in form, since there is no reason to suppose that diverse individuals will have an attachment to their ethnicity. We must therefore enhance channels of communication between citizens politically, through a commitment to a universal ideal of citizenship. This does not necessarily mean, as some advocates of the politics of difference have argued, that all citizens share the same conception of what constitutes the good life. What it does mean, as Oldfield (1990: 25) argues, is that 'the good life for one is not necessarily the good life for another, but the good life for each must include activity which sustains the political community'. Linkages between citizens in the form of reciprocal rights and responsibilities underpin the political community in at least two ways. First, they build solidarity between the members of a society. It is important here to distinguish between solidarity between diverse individuals joined together by the institutions of governance and a stifling conformity that some communitarian theories imply. Second, the exercise of citizenship is an educative process. Individuals learn about the techniques of politics through practising them. This means recognising the close relationship between citizenship and democracy. Indeed, citizenship can be seen as a precondition of democracy. Even if not formally constituted, rights and responsibilities are implied by a democratic system of governance. Democracy involves the idea of equal rights to participate. It also implies those civil rights that are necessary to the expression of opinion such as the right to free speech, association and protest. Conversely, democracy transforms membership of a polity from subjecthood into citizenship. It is only by recognising individuals as autonomous agents capable of self-governance that active citizenship is possible.

In the context of contemporary social conditions, democracy becomes all the more important to stable governance. One of the positive contributions postmodern theory has made to social science is to help to expose the teleological assumptions that underpin many modernist theories of human emancipation. Thus, classical Marxism embraces a theory of change that romanticises one social group – the proletariat – and postulates an end to history where the need for politics and citizenship to mediate between conflicting positions disappears. However, the inevitable victims of revolution are individual rights. For as Engels contends, 'a revolution is certainly the most authoritarian thing there is' (Marx and Engels 1962: 639). Postmodernism, in contrast, has emphasised the socially constructed nature of truth claims. A logical implication of this is to defend the institutions of democracy as the only possible method for reconciling differences and arriving at policy decisions that the majority of the population can live with. Democracy does not aim at a universal truth, but seeks instead to build relationships between diverse citizens. Postmodernists are right to be concerned with perfectionist theories of politics, if perfectionism means that political deliberation aims at a final solution to human conflicts which denies difference. This problem need not arise however if we see perfectionism as meaning that humans are not limited by their natures but are capable of adapting creatively to their changing environment and directing change through democracy. Democracy replaces teleological or evolutionary theories as the means to emancipation, which must be an ongoing and dynamic process.

The precise nature of rights and responsibilities must also be negotiated democratically. However, a relational view of democracy implies that the majority cannot simply ride roughshod over minorities. Democracy cannot involve zero sum games if it is to retain its inclusive character. Instead we must look to accommodate the various voices in society and look to be as inclusive as possible. This necessarily entails a respect for civil and political rights. There is the danger, however, that in liberal societies individuals will choose not to exercise their political rights and the basis of common institutions will thereby be undermined. If we adopt a narrow, rational choice model of human behaviour then such an option may seem entirely reasonable to the individual: the individual decides that his or her contribution is at best marginal and therefore it will make little sense for them to participate. This is certainly a risk in countries like the USA, where in recent years presidents have been elected with only a quarter of the registered voters supporting them. The evidence clearly suggests that whole swathes of American society are alienated from their political institutions (Dalton 1996: 269–71). Partly the problem is the nature of political institutions within liberal society. Most work at a great distance from the individual and make the choice not to exercise one's rights a tempting option. There is, therefore, a strong case for more experiments in new forms of participation which devolve power locally and which are more deliberative and intensive than merely voting. One example of this is citizens' juries, which have been tried with notable success in Britain, the USA and Germany. These juries allow ordinary people to deliberate and give policy advice to governmental agents in policy areas such as health care and education. Thus in Britain, for example, such juries have been used by local authorities to address questions of how NHS

(National Health Service) services might be rationed in a just way. Sometimes such juries have been made up of individuals particularly affected by the policy under discussion. In Fife in Scotland, for example, the charity Age Concern has established a panel of people who are over 75 years of age to consider questions related to the services provided by health workers, the voluntary sector and social workers. The panel members set their own agenda and consider such questions as hospitals' policy on discharging patients. This deliberation resulted in a 14-point plan on what constitutes good practice and was so well received that it was used to underpin policy on hospital discharges in Fife (Ivory 1998: 13).

While there are clearly dangers with allowing public policy to be shaped only by those directly affected by a particular decision, the experience of such juries has been encouraging in that participants experience a sense of empowerment that is often lacking in minimalist models of participation such as voting. Citizens' juries have also produced well-considered and insightful policy suggestions and are just one example of how experiments in deliberation can encourage the ethic of participation so central to a thick sense of citizenship.

As well as reforming political institutions, we do need to address the relationship between political rights and responsibilities. To conclude this section I will consider two proposals that follow logically from the general comments I have made on citizenship and political community, and that provide illustrations of the kind of policy change that a relational view of citizenship might entail. First is the question of compulsory voting, which some countries such as Australia already insist upon. The advantage of compulsory voting is that it recognises the need for rights to be exercised if they are to have substance. In such crucial areas such as deciding upon our representatives it could be argued that by choosing not to vote ourselves we effectively undermine the significance of the right for others

(Dagger 1997). Compulsory voting is a good example of how rights and responsibilities are closely related; for the right to retain its significance, we have a responsibility to cast our vote.

Arguments against compulsory voting are normally of two kinds. The first argument is that compulsion violates an individual's right not to take part in the process, whether because of apathy or out of protest. Second, compulsory voting would give politicians the excuse to ignore what amounts to a 'donkey' vote where people have to be led by their ears to the polling booth! However, the first objection is met by the argument that voting is a civic responsibility as well as an individual right. Moreover, we could allow individuals to register their dissatisfaction by including the option of 'none of the above' on the ballot paper. The argument that by compelling people to vote is to undermine its significance is not a convincing one. In fact, there is a good chance that an element of compulsion would encourage citizens to participate politically in other ways and to ensure that they are politically informed. Currently, politicians are able to ignore many citizens' preferences because these citizens opt out of elections. Levels of non-participation are also closely linked to socio-economic status. The danger is that parties will increasingly ignore the needs of the poorer sections of society and will gear their policies towards satisfying the middle class. Compulsory voting would address the problem of inequalities in participation and would mean that parties could not ignore the millions of citizens who currently do not take part in elections.

Another policy which would address the balance between rights and responsibilities is that of community service (Barber 1984, Dauenhauer 1996). Many countries do require citizens to perform national service in the armed forces. There is no reason why the principle of devoting some time to the community's needs should not be extended to other areas of social life. These might include offering support to the disabled or the elderly, contributing to the maintenance of the environment, or working to enhance the community's cultural activities. The important point is that community service would build solidarity between citizens, particularly if it was designed in such a way as to ensure a good social mix occurred between classes and ethnic groups. Community service would help maintain the civic community and provide valuable services to citizens. As Dauenhauer argues (1996: 160), community service would also be an important aspect of the education for citizenship which society needs to provide for its citizens. Dauenhauer proposes a year of service directly after school as a bridge between childhood and the adult world. It certainly would be important to link community service closely to educational programmes on citizenship, which should be compulsory during school years and which should also play some part in higher education as well. Currently the emphasis in education tends to be towards individual self-development and preparation for work. Education needs also to build civic responsibility and a sense of sociability.

Ideally of course, citizenship responsibilities should take the form of voluntary obligations. However, obligation does not develop in a vacuum. Community is the structural context of individual agency and as such it is hardly unreasonable to expect all citizens to take some responsibility for its maintenance. Critics worry that such duties as compulsory voting and community service are a violation of individual liberty. However, individual liberty is more likely to be imperilled by a one-sided view of citizenship that stresses only abstract rights. Once we accept that our rights depend on maintaining common institutions, we are more likely to accept the need for an enhancement of duty. The kinds of proposals I have discussed here would hardly destroy individual choice. The fact is that in liberal societies the polity makes very few demands on our time. Apart from the duty to obey the law, pay our taxes, and possibly serve on a jury, citizens have few duties to perform. It is nonetheless right to be concerned if greater responsibilities come at the expense of rights. If citizenship is to be enhanced, we must address the question of social rights as well.

RETHINKING SOCIAL RIGHTS

As well as having the opportunity and the responsibility to participate politically, citizens also require the resources to enable them to participate. The community has a duty to provide for every citizen's basic needs. According to Marshall's (1992) liberal account of citizenship, the state accepted this responsibility in the post-war period through the institutionalisation of social rights. The welfare state was to guarantee that no one, regardless of his or her condition of employment, would live in poverty. The rights of social security would ensure that capitalism was civilised and inequalities legitimised. Social rights, for Marshall, give citizenship real substance because they ground citizenship upon publicly funded resources. However, social rights have always had an uneasy relationship with the other rights of citizenship. Barbalet (1988: 67) has argued that we must question whether 'social rights can be rights of citizenship'. He sees citizenship as 'rights of participation' in the polity. Social rights are a means to facilitate this participation, rather than a constitutive part of citizenship as such. In addition, 'citizenship rights are necessarily universal. Social rights, on the other hand, are only meaningful when they are substantive; and substantive rights can never be universal'. Lastly, because social rights depend upon a bureau-cratic and fiscal basis they are not rights at all, but instead are 'conditional opportunities'.

Certainly, social rights are deeply flawed in the form that they have taken in capitalist society. Barbalet is right to identify a tension between an ethic of participation, which is intrinsic to citizenship, and the passive nature of social rights as constituted by the welfare state. The implementation of social rights has depended upon arbitrary and discriminatory decisions of welfare providers. Means-tested benefits in particular, such as income support, have consequently been seen by many recipients not as rights of citizenship but as state hand-outs. Social rights have often stigmatised recipients rather than empowered them. Many social benefits therefore go unclaimed. The administrative decisions that are associated with social rights have had negative implications for individuals' civil rights as calls to crack down on benefit fraud mean harsher and more intrusive policing of benefits. In turn, the whole status of social rights is diminished. Social rights, as constituted in the welfare state, fail to build bridges between citizens. Instead, they create divisions between active citizens, who are able to exercise their market rights through employment, and 'passive' citizens who are constantly labelled as 'undeserving' or members of an 'underclass'.

We do not have to accept Barbalet's argument that social rights are inherently in tension with civil and political rights however. The key to understanding why social rights have failed to achieve the functions that liberals like Marshall hoped for, is that social rights have been understood as supportive rather than subversive to the logic of capitalism. The link between citizenship and the welfare state that emerged after 1945 was therefore comparatively a weak one. The primary relationship between individuals is seen as market interaction governed by contract, rather than the reciprocal relationship of rights and responsibilities. Social rights have tended to be seen as compensation for unemployment, rather than as an intrinsic part of citizenship. The linkage between paid employment and social rights has meant that social citizenship has been biased towards men, who are more likely to be in full-time work and are thereby able to claim the higher rates of benefit associated with graduated tax contributions. Social rights are not inherently selective as Barbalet argues. It is the link between work and social benefits that creates this impression. The third tension between social rights and 'citizenship rights' that Barbalet identifies reveals that the logic of his position is underpinned by an assumption that civil and political rights are in some sense prior to community. To argue that social rights are resource-dependent is of course true. But this is the case for all rights. It is only if we accept the abstract logic of liberalism, which privileges and naturalises those rights that underpin market relations, that we are able to argue that social rights are of a different nature from the other rights of citizenship.

The danger of reifying civil and political citizenship and denying their necessary linkage to social rights is that social rights become extremely vulnerable to erosion. Indeed, following the neo-liberal backlash against social welfare in the 1980s and 1990s, a huge literature has developed on the crisis of the welfare state (see Pierson 1998). Concerns about the negative influence a culture of dependency has upon morality, the detrimental effect high taxation supposedly has for business competitiveness and the problems of an ageing population have all been high on the political agenda in Western societies. Cox (1998) detects a significant weakening of the relationship between welfare benefits and citizenship, even in the most advanced welfare systems. This is somewhat ironic as politicians such as Tony Blair and Bill Clinton have made great use of the language of citizenship in their attempts to plot a 'third way' to govern society that avoids the statism of socialism and the market fundamentalism of neo-liberalism (Giddens 1998). However, the language of citizenship as used by advocates of the third way often plays down rights as unconditional claims and instead maintains that rights can be denied to those who do not accept duties, primarily to work or at least to seek work. This once again highlights the weakness of a social rights regime that is subordinate to market imperatives. If social rights rest upon the willingness to work then logically those wealthy enough to avoid work also avoid their responsibility to the community.

Responsibilities then become stratified on the basis of wealth. As Jordan (1989: 82) contends, 'the only way to create a citizenship obligation to work would be to create a common interest in the provision of certain goods through all contributing part of their working lives to producing this good'. The weak connection between entitlements administered by the welfare state and political citizenship makes social rights vulnerable to the kind of discursive strategies deployed by politicians eager to cut back welfare bills and to maintain their economy's competitive edge in the 'global' market place. If social rights are to have a more secure basis, we must rethink the function they serve and their relationship to citizenship more broadly. Social rights take on a very different form from the welfare rights defined by Marshall and Barbalet if we prioritise the political and egalitarian relationship of citizenship over the unequal market relationships of contract. A proposal that seems to meet many of Barbalet's concerns about social rights is that of a citizens' income (CI). The rest of this section will be devoted to exploring this idea.

CI, sometimes referred to as basic income, is a guaranteed sum of money paid to each adult citizen (with perhaps a lower rate for children) regardless of their employment status. It would be funded by taxation on businesses and individuals. The first advantage of CI is that it is a social right that is universal. It therefore meets the second of Barbalet's concerns about what he sees as the inherently selective nature of social rights. In terms of enhancing citizenship, the significance of CI is not so much that it detaches income from work but rather that it frees citizenship from market constraints. As Esping-Anderson (1990: 21) has remarked, 'the outstanding criterion of social rights must be the degree to which they permit people to make their living standards independently of pure market forces'. CI seems the policy most likely to achieve a decommodification of social rights. In addition, because it is a universal right, once constituted, CI would be likely to be more secure than those social rights that are linked more clearly to shifts in employment patterns. The object of public policy may thereby move towards sustaining the conditions that promote good citizenship rather than designing social and economic policies that serve the market.

Parker (1998: 162) argues that another consequence of decommodifying social citizenship may be a less productionist society, since people would not depend upon environmentally destructive employment to satisfy their basic needs. Reorganising the priorities of society on the basis of political membership rather than market criteria may also lead to more ecologically sound economic management.

What about Barbalet's argument concerning the relationship between social rights and participation? Some advocates of the citizens' income meet this challenge by linking CI to the performance of responsibilities, such as the kind of community service I have advocated. However, by making CI conditional in this way is to risk recreating the problems associated with welfare for work programmes: the wealthy can simply opt out of the scheme. I would argue instead that CI should be paid in recognition of the community's duty to meet its members' basic needs. If citizenship is an expression of the relationship between the individual and community, then CI would reflect the importance placed upon this relationship by showing that the community's priorities are the welfare of its members, rather than the needs of the market. CI has the distinct advantage over other methods of social rights because it recognises and enhances both interdependence *and* individual autonomy.

The payment of CI would more readily recognise the social nature of wealth creation. The dominance of neo-liberalism, which attributes wealth creation primarily to dynamic entrepreneurs and individual initiative, would be challenged by a social policy based upon shared membership of a political community. Moreover, as Hirst (1994: 182) contends, 'if wealth is, in large measure, social, then poverty cannot be made an entirely individual stigma'. CI would help to share the benefits of society more fairly.

One of the problems with conventional social rights is that not only are they tied closely to work, but that the definition of useful work is very narrow. This is partly why women benefit less from conventional welfare schemes. The disproportionate amounts of time women spend on unpaid domestic work and social care go largely unrecognised and are undervalued. What is more, because of the unequal structure of the labour market, women are less likely to have made enough contributions to claim those benefits which are related to income. For example, in Britain in 1991 only 15 per cent of women claiming state pension had paid enough contributions to receive a full pension of £52 per week (Parker 1993: vii). CI would considerably improve the lot of many women by implicitly recognising their contributions to society. It would give women greater resources which may be used to purchase the time necessary to participate politically. CI also treats women as autonomous individuals, rather than in terms of their marriage status, sexuality or family relationships. As the nuclear family, dominated by a male bread-winner, becomes more uncommon, CI is a social policy that is sensitive to social changes in family structures. Lister (1997: 189) worries that CI might inadvertently reinforce men's economic advantage over women by tying women more closely to domestic duties. This does not necessarily follow however. CI does not preclude other social policy measures designed to equalise the roles of men and women, and no one policy can address all possible inequalities.

Barbalet's third point about social rights is that they are dependent upon bureaucratic decisions which may discriminate in the implementation of benefits. CI would have considerable practical advantages in this regard. It would greatly simplify the tax and benefit system, which in most countries is complex and confusing. CI would be relatively easy to administer and cutting welfare bureaucracy would make great savings. CI would also remove recipients' dependence upon the decisions of state officials. Because it is a universal benefit, it would be enjoyed as a basic right of citizenship and would carry no stigma.

Despite the advantages of CI over conventional methods for delivering social rights, Pixley (1993) is nonetheless right to stress that by itself CI is no panacea. Unless CI is accompanied by a devolution of power and the democratisation of the state and economy, CI might be in effect hijacked by the state. By this Pixley means that CI might be employed cynically by a state eager to avoid solving the problems of unemployment and keen to reduce the obligations it has to its members. For Pixley, capitalist society can only be transformed by market participation through work. By basing social policy on CI, we risk marginalising many citizens and leaving the capitalist labour contract unreformed. Moreover, it is through work that obligations and networks of communication between individuals develop. For this reason, Pixley (ibid.: 199) argues that

> a nexus between pay and work is a less decisive political and social issue than the nexus between citizenship and paid work. That is, the basic conditions for political participation in modern societies are strongly linked to mainstream employment.

Pixley's arguments however fail to address the problem of the shift away from full employment, which characterised the post-war Fordist system of production, to more flexible and part-time employment patterns in the 1980s and 1990s. Provided people's needs are met, we need not necessarily condemn such a shift in the labour market. Pixley rather underestimates the alienating elements of work for many people. CI would free people from much alienating and energy-sapping work that does much to undermine active citizenship for people who lack the time to fully exercise their rights and responsibilities. However, it is certain that the vast majority of people would still wish to be usefully employed. There is simply no evidence for the existence of a dependency culture that the neo-liberal right has popularised. But CI would allow a balance to be struck between employment and other activities, many of which are central to the practice of citizenship such as lifelong education, voluntary work and political participation. By releasing people from dependency upon employers, pressure would also be applied on employers to adopt more worker-friendly policies that are more able to meet the diverse needs of citizens.

In terms of social rights, CI seems the most likely to provide a stable basis for citizenship. Some critics point to the economic unfeasibility of such a policy. However, such arguments have always been used against universal benefits. For example, when the NHS was formed in Britain after the Second World War, many conservatives in particular questioned its financial feasibility. The key point is that CI *is* viable if the political will exists to implement it. The real question is how much do we value citizenship? Are we prepared to sacrifice our rights and responsibilities in the name of narrow economic criteria? This is the challenge that recognising the material basis of citizenship sets us. Van Parijs (1995: 232) argues cogently that CI is the 'centrepiece of a just socio-economic regime'. By removing the condition that individuals should seek often undignified and exploitative employment from social rights, CI forms an essential part of a conception of citizenship that addresses people's non-material, as well as material needs. As Meadows et al. argue, 'people do not need enormous cars; they need respect' (cit. in Twine 1994: 83). A social policy with CI at its heart is most likely to satisfy this requirement.

Of course, CI would initially be limited to members of a particular political community. The problem of inequalities across societies is not addressed by such a policy. However, before I move on to consider such problems in chapter 6 I shall conclude this chapter with an examination of the idea of intimate citizenship.

INTIMATE CITIZENSHIP

Another area in which citizenship might be enhanced is conveyed by Ken Plummer's (1999) useful phrase, 'intimate citizenship'. In my reading of the term, intimate citizenship refers to the application of the principles of citizenship to interpersonal relationships. In the liberal tradition, citizenship has been seen as a strictly public affair, where reason holds sway. The private sphere is based on family life (the realm of human emotion) and market exchanges that are governed by the laws of supply and demand. In the discussion of social rights above, I have already suggested that a citizenship subservient to market imperatives is undermined. The introduction of CI would be a major step towards tackling this problem. Here I want to discuss how the idea of citizenship can be applied to such questions as family relationships and the management of violence.

Effectively the private sphere is depoliticised in liberal theory. It is the sharp divide between a political public world and a non-political private realm that has been challenged by feminists. The slogan 'the personal is political' captures nicely the idea that the private realm does involve power relationships that are deeply political. Moreover, a sharp divide between private and public is itself a political construct that favours men's interests. Such a divide has the effect, feminists argue, of hiding from public gaze the violence, particularly towards women and children, that often occurs in family life. An important aspect of a holistic citizenship is the application of its ideals to this private sphere. This does not mean that the relationships entailed by citizenship form the totality of human relations. Neither does it mean dispensing with a public–private divide completely. There is a good case, however, for applying the idea of reciprocal rights and responsibilities to human relationships in general. A deep sense of citizenship does imply that we cannot have a sharp divide between our identity as human on the one hand and citizen on the other. In a different context, this was very much the point that Marx was driving at in his *On the Jewish Question*. The idea that the rights and responsibilities of citizenship can be limited to a narrow set of human relationships risks undermining the importance of citizenship completely. We cannot rationally deliberate and compromise in a public assembly and then return home to abuse our family. A citizenship beyond liberalism is more demanding than that. It requires us to respect the rights of all of those with whom we have relations, and to honour our responsibilities towards them.

Such questions are inevitably raised by the development of more individualistic and yet egalitarian societies. As such, a holistic approach to citizenship is consistent with the core principles of liberalism. As women, sexual minorities and other previously excluded groups struggle for recognition, the public–private divide is inevitably problematised. At times, the relationship between public and private seems even paradoxical. In a discussion of citizenship and sexuality, Weeks (1998: 37) expresses this point very well:

> the sexual citizen then makes a claim to transcend the limits of the personal sphere by going public, but the going public is, in a necessary but paradoxical move, about protecting the possibilities of private life and private choice in a more inclusive society.

What this means is that we cannot assume a neat, unchanging divide between the personal and political. In fact, such a divide presupposes exclusion and the suffocation of legitimate claims to rights. The struggle homosexuals have had, first to have their sexuality decriminalised, and then to seek equality with heterosexuals, is a good example of what were traditionally private questions of morality entering the public domain.

A closely related point, and a crucial component of intimate citizenship, is the democratisation of the private sphere. Two writers who have considered this question are Giddens and Hoffman. Giddens (1998: 93) is in little doubt that 'the family is becoming democratised' and in ways which are closely related to processes of democratisation generally. Greater equality between men and women and more sensitivity to the rights of children inevitably lead to a renegotiation of personal relationships based on principles of deliberation and, crucially, 'freedom from violence'. Ideas of rights and responsibilities pervade these relationships, whether rights and responsibilities are formalised in law or not. Giddens believes that social policy must aim to firm up intimate citizenship by providing a network of rights and responsibilities between family members. For example, he suggests that as more couples are having children outside of marriage, what is required is a contractual commitment to children that is separate from the marriage contract. Such a contract would give both parents equal responsibility for their children's welfare.

Giddens contends that, by applying the ideas of citizenship to personal relationships, we raise questions about the role of violence in social life generally. By gearing social policy towards encouraging compromise between individuals, we create a political framework that can work to remove violence from *all* human relationships. As Giddens (1994: 119) writes,

> individuals who have a good understanding of their own emotional makeup, and who are able to communicate effectively with others on a personal basis, are likely to be well prepared for wider tasks of citizenship. Communication skills developed within the arenas of personal life might very well be generalizable across wider contexts.

Despite making close analogies between personal relationships and public life, Giddens is nevertheless unwilling to follow the logic of his theory: a critique of violence in human relationships should lead us to a critique of the state. Giddens is trapped in a dualistic logic that refuses to go beyond a static view of the public and private. On the one hand, he sees the way in which violence within the family destroys reciprocity and democracy. On the other hand, he maintains that a society without the state, which rests its power upon violence, would lead only to chaos. Indeed, Giddens (ibid.: 125) appears to see violence, or at least the threat of violence, as the only basis for social order. He writes 'where states have no enemies, but face only diffuse threats, a potentially but not actually hostile international environment, disintegrative tendencies internally might again become strong'. In direct contrast to his plea for democratic families, Giddens is arguing here that to ensure peace, states must prepare for war!

John Hoffman's (1995) ideas have been ground-breaking because he has made the necessary link between the state and human relationships in general, which Giddens, because of his statist assumptions, refuses to make. Hoffman argues that for citizenship to fulfil its emancipatory potential, it is necessary to move beyond the state. This is because the democratic ideals closely associated with citizenship oppose violent solutions to political problems which the state, with its claim to a monopoly of force, implicitly endorses. The use of violence is relational in its effect because it dehumanises the perpetuator as well as the victim. As Hoffman (1998: 174) writes:

> It is not simply that the administrators of violence brutalize themselves when they use violence against others . . . In a state-centred society, every individual knows that all laws are underpinned by physical force which comes into effect if all else fails. This makes it impossible for anyone to comply with norms in a way which is not at the same time contaminated by a fear of violence.

Tensions between what is public and what is private are inevitable, argues Hoffman. What is crucial, however, is that these tensions are resolved democratically and not by force. The democratisation implied by intimate citizenship, and the development of more representative political institutions and new forms of political participation are all part of the same movement towards a post-statist citizenship. Central to Hoffman's theory is a distinction between force and coercion. Force involves the negation of choice. Coercion on the other hand refers to non-violent social pressures that may be aimed at individuals who refuse to respect others' rights and who display anti-social behaviour. Critics may argue that this aspect of Hoffman's theory is utopian. However, Hoffman's theory meets the charge of utopianism on at least three counts. The first way in which Hoffman's theory points realistically towards a progressive future for citizenship beyond the state relates to the question of globalisation, which is creating a momentum towards global systems of governance. In the next chapter, I will consider how citizenship can be reconceptualised in this new global context.

Second, by problematising the relationship between democracy and the state, Hoffman's theory implies that any movement towards democracy undermines the state's reliance upon force. The state does not disappear overnight but it is nonetheless increasingly challenged by the process of democratisation both within the personal and the global spheres. Third, by accepting the need for coercion that falls short of force, Hoffman allows for the fact that all societies have norms and values which govern social interaction and which require some form of regulation. Of course, some value systems are conservative and oppressive. However, like the question of the public–private divide, the key to addressing this problem is to ensure that the mechanisms through which norms are decided and put into practice are democratic and deliberative. It is true that all societies, whether they are governed by a state or not, require constraints upon members' activities. Hoffman's argument that stable government requires social coercion does not violate individual liberty but is an important aspect of freedom, where freedom is conceived in social terms. The consistency of Hoffman's theory with liberal principles is supported by the fact that liberals such as J. S. Mill (1974) hold similar views on the role of social pressure which falls short of actual force. In his famous tract *On Liberty*, Mill argues that we must respect the rights of others to choose how to lead their lives as a matter of principle. However, this does not prevent us from applying pressure upon an individual who is acting in a way that may harm themselves or others. Indeed, in many cases we are morally obliged to try to persuade others that their actions may have negative consequences. More recently, communitarians have also stressed the importance of informal constraints upon citizens' actions. Etzioni (1997: 120) contends that the measure of good societies is the 'extent to which they rely on informal social mechanisms and what I call the moral voice, versus on the state and its coercive tools of law enforcement'.

The idea of coercion as used by Hoffman can be conceptually linked to the ethic of care, which many feminists have advocated as a way of civilising citizenship. This is possible because Hoffman clearly has a view of coercion that is constructive and compassionate, rather than narrow-minded and moralistic in the negative sense of the term. A positive view of coercion, as a concern for others' welfare, is therefore close to the ideal of care. By introducing notions of care and compassion into debates concerning intimate citizenship, feminists seek to bridge the dualism between reason and emotion which so concerns post-modern critics of liberalism. Bubeck's (1995) view is that, while we must avoid naturalising women's behaviour, it is nevertheless the case that women's experiences of mothering and caring for dependants in general make them more likely than men to have a relational view of politics that is sensitive to others' needs and concerns. Bubeck (ibid.: 27) argues that 'both care and politics are "muddling through" types of activities which involve the welfare of others'. An ethic of care also implies interdependence rather than the abstract form of independence advanced by liberalism. As such, by bringing the values of care to citizenship we are more likely to build consensual relationships in both the public and private domains. Critics like Ignatieff (1991) are right to be concerned about linking care to citizenship if this means neglecting the question of formal social rights. Nonetheless, when Ignatieff (ibid.: 34) writes that 'welfare is about rights, not caring' he presents us with a false choice. A purely formal expression of rights can easily lead us into the abstract logic of instrumentalism that sees no connection between our rights and our obligations to others. The challenge that intimate citizenship presents us is to combine a strengthening of traditional expressions of rights and responsibilities in formal terms with a sense of compassion and obligation that informs all relationships in both the public and private worlds.

In this chapter, I have presented some ways in which citizenship can be enhanced and the strengths of liberalism such as individual rights and equality built upon. Rights and responsibilities must be reformed to allow diverse individuals who nonetheless share an interest in the maintenance of common institutions, to build a sense of solidarity and mutual endeavour. I have suggested that in the increasingly individualistic context of liberal society, we should be required to perform more duties than is currently the case in many communities. Compulsory voting and community service are examples that may encourage the ethic of participation, which I have argued is crucial to a coherent definition of citizenship. Experiments in deliberative methods of policy-making such as citizens' juries are another way in which political rights can be made more meaningful and collaborative. A holistic approach to citizenship must also acknowledge, however, that an effective ethic of participation must be supported by a material foundation. Traditional approaches to social rights have failed to secure individual autonomy. In contrast, a citizens' income is a policy that removes citizenship's dependence upon the market and decommodifies rights in ways which are likely to encourage a more activist and progressive citizenry. Finally, I have argued that a thick conception of citizenship requires us to rethink our personal as well as public relationships. Developing intimate citizenship is crucial to the further democratisation of society and to the conceptualisation of a citizenship beyond the state.

6

CITIZENSHIP IN A GLOBAL AGE

Globalisation has, like citizenship, become a buzzword of late modernity. The popularity of the concept is reflected in the proliferation of articles, books and political speeches exploring the notion that a combination of advanced communications systems, the growth of world markets, and the pervasive reach of multinational corporations (MNCs) are steadily eroding the boundaries that have hitherto defined social membership. Could it be that the concept of citizenship is becoming redundant, since its close association historically with closed political communities is inappropriate to the porous boundaries of a new global age? We have seen how defenders of nationality such as Miller (1995) contend that without the psychological barriers between citizen and stranger that a distinct national culture provides, citizenship can be no more than a superficial concept, which is unlikely to engender the values of civic virtue necessary to good governance. In sum, globalisation appears to challenge the contemporary relevance of citizenship because it blurs the boundaries, both material and psychological, which have made citizenship significant in modernity.

In the first section of this chapter, I analyse the impact globalisation is having upon citizenship. While the economic and cultural effects of globalisation are often exaggerated or misinterpreted, globalisation, particularly in the form of planetary risks, has indeed hung a question mark over traditional assumptions about social membership. In particular, the tension between universal rights and sovereignty (which has set the limits of citizenship within modernity), is being highlighted by these processes. Traditional international relations theory is unable to conceptualise the nature of contemporary social changes that are creating a more interdependent world. We must therefore move beyond traditional conceptions of security if we are to remodel citizenship in a way that is relevant to the requirements of a global age.

Some authors, such as Yasemin Soysal (1994), have suggested that in the context of globalisation, citizenship is being replaced by human rights; the protection of these universal rights is now the key to securing individual autonomy. The second part of the chapter addresses the question of whether human rights are indeed superseding citizenship in the way that Soysal suggests. I argue that human rights cannot replace citizenship, because governance requires the exercise of political participation and responsibilities as well as the preservation of rights. Finally, I explore the relationship between governance and citizenship and consider whether citizenship has a future in a global age. I argue that pressure to enhance citizenship within states, though by itself important, must be accompanied by efforts to build multiple sites of governance that seek to fulfil the egalitarian logic of liberal citizenship in ways which reach beyond the limits of the state.

GLOBALISATION AND CITIZENSHIP

Globalisation is generally said to involve processes of social change which are cultural, economic and political in form. Waters (1995: 3) provides a succinct definition of globalisation: 'a social process in which the constraints of geography on social and political arrangements recede and in which people become increasingly aware they are receding'.

Innovations in information and communications technology, including satellites, computers, jet travel and digital television, have made access to other cultures easier and more instantaneous than in previous eras. A consequence of this, argues Ohmae (1995), is the development of a global culture that is moving people beyond narrow national self-interests. As consumers of cultural symbols and signs, as well as material products, individuals are now looking beyond the boundaries of the state and making choices according to personal taste rather than national identity. The world of the global consumer is facilitated by the growth in world trade and the constitution of a global market place. The principal vehicle of these market forces is the multinational company, which is increasingly breaking its links with the state and is instead seeking new opportunities across the globe, regardless of the dictates of national interest. The significance of the rise of multinationals is, however, disputed by those who consider globalisation as a concept to be ill defined and overstated. Hirst and Thompson (1996), for example, have presented a critique of the idea of economic globalisation. They argue persuasively that world trade and investment patterns are still heavily concentrated within Europe, Japan and the USA, and that multinational companies are very much reliant upon the framework of laws, training, education, research, and general infrastructure provided by the state.

Additionally, polarisation, rather than globalisation, may best describe aspects of world trade, since whole regions are more or less excluded from the benefits of capital accumulation. Countries in Africa, Latin America and Eastern Europe for instance have in recent years seen their share of world markets decline. Such evidence contradicts the optimistic account of globalisation presented by Ohmae, who considers the triumph of capitalism on a planetary scale to bring benefits for all. The reality is that it is Western states that are benefiting from the liberalisation of trade in many areas. Moreover, in areas of commerce such as the control of technological innovations and copyright, where the West has a vested interest in maintaining control, tight regulations remain. Korten (1995: 180–1) highlights how, for example, international patent rights have been extended to genetic materials such as seeds and natural medicinals which means that 'a few companies have effectively obtained monopoly rights over genetic research on an entire species and on any useful products of that research'. For these reasons, then, there is a lot of truth in the argument that globalisation, rather than marking the end of the state, in fact represents a particular state strategy that aims at securing the interests of political and economic elites of liberal states.

There is also good reason to doubt the thesis that Ohmae presents concerning global culture. In effect, Ohmae's idea of global culture represents the spread of liberal values of individualism, market forces and Western consumer tastes. Many cultures have in fact responded negatively to the apparent triumph of liberalism following the ending of the cold war. Often these reactions take the form of fundamentalist reactions to what is perceived as the superficial and unsatisfying values of consumer capitalism. The rise of Islamic fundamentalism in parts of Africa and Asia, the huge range of ethnic conflict in the ex-Soviet Union and Eastern Europe, and the continued dominance of the communist party in China are all evidence that contradicts any simple global culture thesis (Faulks 1999: 53–70).

Fukuyama is another commentator who sees in globalisation the triumph of liberal values. In Fukuyama's case, however, it is processes of democratisation in such regions as Asia, Africa and Eastern Europe, as well as the spread of market principles, which are cited as evidence that the alternatives to liberal democracy are collapsing:

> Liberal democracy remains the only coherent political aspiration that spans different regions and cultures around the globe. In addition, liberal principles in economics – the 'free market' – have spread, and have succeeded in producing unprecedented levels of material prosperity.
>
> (Fukuyama 1992: xiii)

A consideration of Ohmae's and Fukuyama's arguments helps throw light upon the nature of the processes associated with globalisation in ways that take us back to the internal tensions within liberalism we have identified throughout this book. These tensions have helped shape the form and development of citizenship. Ohmae sees little place for democratic citizenship in his vision of a global age. Like many neo-liberals, Ohmae is highly sceptical of the values of democracy and instead sees the market as the surest way to govern society and to distribute resources. Fukuyama sees a much closer relationship between the values of the market and democracy and believes that the two institutions of capitalism and citizenship in combination create the most favourable conditions for individual freedom and stable government. I have already demonstrated, however, that there are in fact strong contradictions between the values of capitalism and citizenship: where the values of the market are dominant, citizenship acquires a thin and vulnerable status. Globalisation is making this contradiction more acute in several ways.

First, while the world economy cannot actually be described as global in an inclusive sense of the term, it has become more internationalised (Hirst and Thompson 1996). States compete for market shares in an international system that is only minimally governed. Institutions such as the World Bank, Organisation for Economic Co-operation and Development (OECD), and the International Monetary Fund (IMF) attempt to give some structure to the world economy, but overwhelmingly these institutions are dominated by advocates of neo-liberalism. Moreover, some of the most important actors within the economy are subject to weak regulation. The activities of MNCs for example are governed by no international charter and companies have resisted attempts by bodies such as the United Nations (UN) to curtail their activities. For example, the United Nations Centre on Transnational Corporations, which was once a focus for criticism and scrutiny of the activities of MNCs, has been reduced, under pressure from powerful companies, to a 'collecting house for information' (Horsman and Marshall 1995: 97) This lack of regulation of their activities means that powerful MNCs are in a strong position to exploit the need poorer countries have for jobs and foreign investment. Attracting an MNC to one's territory may thereby involve the limitation of democratic scrutiny over the company's activities and a reduction in basic social and civil freedoms, such as rights to welfare and trade union membership. So, as competition between states grows stronger, the tension between state interest and universal rights and between capitalism and democracy becomes more intense.

Second, the dominance of the market over citizenship is an important element in the development of global risks. These risks are the most important aspect of global change. Unlike the advantages of the 'global' market or the values of abstract individualism, risk can truly be said to be planetary in its impact. The idea of global risk refers to problems that cannot be managed successfully by any single state. They include migration, infectious diseases, international crime, nuclear power and ecological damage: none of these problems respect the boundaries that states defend. Modern communications technology has exacerbated these problems and made states and individuals more aware that these problems exist. Migration and crime, for example, are facilitated by improvements in transport systems, while evermore sophisticated television networks beam pictures of the latest refugee crisis or act of terrorism into the homes of ordinary citizens. The development of global risk has huge implications for the role of the state and its ability to guarantee citizenship. In classical international relations theory, the state, which concentrates force in the form of sovereignty, is seen as the only plausible method by which order can be maintained. The primary justification the state has to rule is its promise to provide security to its citizens. It is this Hobbesian logic that is being challenged by contemporary social changes associated with globalisation.

Realists have argued that since states are the only viable institution of governance, the claims of individuals outside of the jurisdiction of any individual state must be balanced by the state's primary duty to its own citizens. In effect, realists postulate an inherent opposition in the international sphere between order and demands for justice. However, with the intensification of planetary risk, this opposition can no longer be sustained. Many of the problems associated with risk are closely related to the high levels of global inequality that exist between states. The processes associated with economic globalisation, as championed by neo-liberals such as Ohmae, have increased this inequality. The deregulated, and therefore unstable, nature of financial markets, for example, impacts negatively upon the maintenance of citizenship rights, particularly in poorer countries. In turn, this leads to greater poverty, which increases the possibility of instability and war. Given the increase in the destructive capability of modern weaponry, warfare is much harder to contain within a single state or even a geographical region. Environmental damage, which is inherently of global importance, is also linked to poverty, as developing states struggle desperately to increase industrial productivity rather than seeking sustainable methods of development that may be less profitable in the short term.

The effects of these inequalities of basic rights and liberties are increasingly impacting directly upon rich as well as poor countries. Migration and international crime are linked to this inequality, for example. The phenomenon of economic refugees, who seek to leave the poor regions of the world and search for a place at the high table, is alarming liberal states. This problem is set to become one of the key political issues of the twenty-first century (Bali 1997). Those who stay in the poorer regions of the world are more likely to be tempted to trade in illegal substances such as drugs because the base price for most legal commodities is kept low by the Western-controlled currency markets. These problems mean that a simple dichotomy between domestic matters and international politics, which realists have argued must be sustained, is increasingly untenable. Booth, in a telling critique of traditional international relations theory, has argued that security interests have tended to be defined in terms of state interests. This approach has in fact masked the real problems of risk that threaten world order. In relation to nuclear deterrence, for example, Booth (1995: 335) writes that much international relations theory has 'employed the euphemistic jargon of nuclear strategy, and [we] have utterly distanced ourselves from the subject matter – the possible extinction of civilisation'.

In the context of globalisation, however, where risks are both more dangerous and more transparent, states cannot convincingly claim to guarantee their own citizens' rights if they do not also consider the rights of individuals in other communities. It is for this reason that some writers are arguing that human rights are replacing citizenship as the primary guarantee of individual autonomy.

HUMAN RIGHTS AND CITIZENSHIP

Yasemin Soysal is one of those who detects an enhanced role for human rights in late modernity. In her book, the *Limits of*

Citizenship, she sets out a compelling argument which has at its centre the assertion that 'a new and more universal concept of citizenship has unfolded in the post-war era, one whose organising and legitimating principles are based on *universal personhood* rather than *national belonging*' (Soysal 1994: 1, emphasis added). The context of this shift is the development of a global system that encompasses international law, the United Nations network, global civil society, and regional governance, as found in institutions such as the European Union.

Consequently, the language of human rights is becoming increasingly central to the government of world affairs, as respect for the person challenges the idea that states are sovereign in relation to their citizens and that other states or international bodies have no right to interfere in this primary relationship. Soysal's evidence for this transformation is focused upon the experience of so-called guest workers in Europe. These are individuals who live and work in a foreign country, often for years, without ever acquiring citizenship status. The growing importance of human rights, however, means that the benefits of citizenship are becoming less important. Organisations representing guest workers have been able to mobilise support for the extension of basic social and civil rights. Thus the significance of citizenship has been reduced to the point where 'noncitizens' rights do not differ significantly from those of citizens' (ibid.: 119). As such, social membership is increasingly postnational and based upon personhood rather than citizenship (ibid.: 44). Even groups such as Muslims, who have historically lived in tension with liberal values, are utilising discourses of human rights in ways which 'speak to "modern individuals' needs"' such as rights to worship and to cultural recognition (ibid.: 116).

Importantly, Soysal rejects arguments that seek to understand the experience of guest workers as beneficiaries of the extension of the territorial reach of citizenship, which now includes denizens as well as citizens by augmenting the criteria for rights based upon nationality with the additional criteria of residency. Such perspectives, contends Soysal (1994: 139), 'remain within the confines of the nation-state model' (see Brubaker 1992). Instead, what is happening to guest workers reflects a more 'profound transformation in the institution of citizenship, both in its institutional logic and in the way it is legitimised. To locate the changes, we need to go beyond the nation-state' (Soysal 1994: 139).

I am in full agreement with Soysal upon the urgent need to reconceptualise citizenship in ways which break the link with the state. It is only in this way that the rights of citizenship can be extended in a manner consistent with liberal notions of the equal worth of individuals. Soysal is also right to identify the growing importance of human rights in world politics. Since the Second World War, international law governing human rights has been expanding rapidly. The UN Declaration of Human Rights, which was adopted unopposed by the UN General Assembly in 1948, is the centrepiece of human rights law. Since then, other conventions covering such matters as the outlawing of torture, discrimination against women and children, and the promotion of the rights of migrants have gained widespread international support (Bretherton 1996: 251). In 1993, 171 governments at the World Conference on Human Rights in Vienna supported a statement to the effect that economic, social and cultural rights are 'universal, indivisible, and interdependent and interrelated' (Broadbent 1997: 6). Moreover, within Europe in particular, cases of injustice within states are increasingly likely to be decided at a level beyond the individual state. An excellent example of this occurred on 27 September 1999, when the European Court of Human Rights in Strasbourg ruled in favour of four gays (three men, one woman) who had objected to the fact that Britain's armed forces exercised a ban on homosexual and lesbian recruits. The Court ruled that the British Government was contravening the basic human right to enjoy a private life, the nature of which should have no bearing upon eligibility for employment.

There is evidence, then, to suggest that states are becoming aware of the problems of global risk and how abuses of human rights by states are likely to impact beyond state boundaries. As Turner (1993) has observed, risk has helped to create common interests and an awareness of the frailty of human existence. Risk has thereby created the basis for a high degree of agreement on the need for human rights. As Turner (1993: 184) puts it, 'frailty is a universal feature of human existence'. For Turner (ibid.: 187), globalisation means that 'the debate about [human] rights might begin to replace the debate about citizenship in both academic and political life'. Does an enhanced role for human rights effectively mark the end of citizenship as a useful concept as both Turner and Soysal imply? An analysis of some of the weaknesses of Soysal's arguments will illustrate that human rights cannot supersede citizenship in the way that she and Turner suggest.

The first problem with Soysal's thesis is that while many guest workers might increasingly enjoy social and civil rights, they do not possess political rights. This is a major problem if, as I have argued, we place great importance upon participation as a defining characteristic of citizenship. While it may be true that immigrant groups have been able to organise themselves politically in the context of civil society, without formal rights to vote or stand for office immigrants can take little part in the formulation and implementation of policies that may impact negatively upon their social entitlements and civil liberties. Non-citizens are therefore objects of state policy rather than active participants.

Human rights by themselves do not ensure the development of the participatory networks that are necessary to sustain common institutions of governance. Such networks are also crucial in building bridges between immigrant groups and the dominant culture within the polity. It is right to seek to detach citizenship from nationality. A postnational model of citizenship, as expressed in Habermas's (1994) notion of constitutional patriotism, nonetheless requires that all members of a community participate in and display loyalty to their governmental institutions. It is hardly healthy for any democracy to have large groups of individuals working and living in a community, but without the opportunity to make decisions about that community's future: membership of a polity involves responsibilities as well as rights. It can only fuel hostility towards minorities if some groups are seen to benefit from the social aspects of citizenship without playing their part in the community. Human rights, then, do not address the question of reciprocity of obligation. Crucially, it is because citizenship involves participation and responsibilities that human rights cannot simply supersede citizenship in the way Soysal suggests. For these reasons, 'non-citizenship is tolerable in the interim, but not in principle' (Joppke 1998: 29).

In any case, Soysal is over-optimistic about the extent to which immigrants do in fact enjoy social and civil rights. Immigrants' standing within the community may well be challenged and undermined by shifts towards more draconian immigration or asylum policies. Hostility to further immigration can undermine the security and rights of a minority already living within the state. Furthermore, as Bhabha has commented,

> Racial harassment and violence persist across EU member states. Discriminatory police behaviour and visible ghettoisation characterise European metropolitan cities. Widespread racism in employment and in the provision of public services remains a matter of acute public concern across the EU. Despite formal legal entitlements to an extensive range of state benefits, in practice, Europe's third country nationals do not enjoy the full civil rights to which the 'native' population has access . . . Such

> evidence rebuts Soysal's optimism that the promotion of human
> rights in Europe is a panacea, resolving the divisiveness that has
> accompanied the delineation of Europe.
>
> (Bhabha 1998: 602–3)

Countries outside Europe conform even less to the postnational
model of citizenship that Soysal outlines. In the USA, for example,
changes in welfare legislation in 1996 limited eligibility of
immigrants to virtually all cash benefits. As Schuck (1998: 192)
remarks, this legalisation has increased 'sharply the value of
American citizenship while reducing the value of permanent
legal resident status'. Schuck also makes the point that there
are around 5 million illegal immigrants in the USA who play a
crucial role in the economy as low-paid factory and domestic
workers. These persons feel little benefit from the postnational
order described by Soysal.

The guest worker's experience in Europe cannot be easily
generalised into a widespread shift to a postnational citizenship.
Joppke (1998: 25) argues that by focusing upon the experience
of these workers, Soysal is in danger of elevating 'the fringe into
the core experience'. Also, in those countries such as Germany
where guest workers are numerous, there is an ongoing debate
over the desirability of denying citizenship to long-standing
residents. In 1999 Chancellor Schröder's Social Democratic
Government passed a new citizenship law which cut the link
between German blood and nationality and thereby paved the
way for guest workers to seek citizenship. The new Act gives
automatic citizenship to children born to foreign residents. This
shows that there is a strong strain of opinion in states like
Germany, with a high number of guest workers, that does
consider it a problem to have millions of non-citizens residing
on a long-term basis in the state. Moreover, Joppke observes that
the vast majority of people do not choose to migrate and rely
upon their own state to protect their rights. However, human

rights are abused by states in many parts of the globe and a stable postnational order will need to address the institutions of governance that guarantee rights globally. This will require a more critical engagement with the powers of the state, if human rights are not to remain secondary to sovereignty. As Joppke (ibid.: 29) contends, 'unless it solves the problem of order, post-national membership must remain either utopian or an anomaly within a world of states'.

The question of human rights cannot then be detached from the wider political question of governance. The central paradox that is shaping world politics in late modernity, and which Soysal (1994: 157) identifies, is 'a deterritorialized expansion of rights despite the territorialized closure of politics'. The point is, however, that human rights rest upon shaky foundations unless mechanisms can be found to move beyond state-orientated definitions of politics. In her eagerness to proclaim a postnational order, Soysal in effect defends a highly abstract view of rights which distances these rights from the social and political structures that sustain them. A sustainable postnational model of citizenship must in fact be more than an abstract defence of human rights, because, as I have argued, governance requires participation and responsibilities as well as rights. In this sense, Soysal can identify the 'limits of citizenship' only because she defines the concept in a very narrow and passive way.

CITIZENSHIP AND GOVERNANCE BEYOND THE STATE

Despite the importance of human rights doctrines, citizenship retains a salience when considering the problem of governance. This is for two main reasons. First is that, although globalisation has altered the context in which states govern, it is the state that remains the institution most able to concentrate economic, military and communicative power (Faulks 1999). The state therefore forms the primary context for the individual citizen. Rights and responsibilities are still exercised mainly at the level of the state. International actors such as MNCs and bodies like the World Bank and the IMF are not rootless actors but rely upon a frameworks of rules determined by states. This means that diverse strategies towards citizenship are likely to continue, and this means pressure to enhance citizenship will need to be aimed at further democratising states in ways in which the values of citizenship – such as equality – are extended within state boundaries. Examples of the kind of reforms I have in mind have been set out in chapter 5. Second, citizenship expresses a relationship between rights, responsibilities and participation which is crucial to any form of governance. The problem with human rights is that they are not tied to the idea of political community and lack effective mechanisms through which they can be fulfilled. Rights, of themselves, are unlikely to create the appropriate context for social order. The arguments of Soysal and Turner, then, who advocate the replacement of citizenship by human rights, based upon the recognition of personhood in the case of Soysal, or human frailty in Turner's account, would leave us with a very passive model of rights and do not address the need for reciprocal responsibilities.

Moreover, not all analysts of international politics accept the arguments advanced by Soysal and Turner that universal rights are sustainable or even desirable. Recently, Samuel Huntington (1998) has breathed new life into a state-centred model of world order by arguing that the pursuit of universal standards of justice, in the form of human rights, is counterproductive. Huntington's neo-realism represents a second possible strategy to the question of how we understand the relationship between citizenship and globalisation that contrasts starkly with the human rights model. Huntington maintains that since the world is divided into distinct civilisations, which are mutually and inevitably suspicious of one another, it would be impossible to ground global governance on the foundation of universal human rights. Instead, 'the security of the world requires acceptance of global multi-culturality' (Huntington 1998: 318). The chief protectors of these civilisations are states. Therefore, attempts to undermine sovereignty through the promotion of human rights are likely to lead only to further conflict. For Huntington, the communications technology of the global age has accentuated rather than diminished the differences between cultures.

Huntington is motivated by a fear of the rise of aggressive alternatives to liberalism in the form of fundamentalism, and in particular militant Islam. What Huntington fails to fully acknowledge, however, is the far more dangerous impact of *Western fundamentalism* in the form of neo-liberalism. It is an obsession with liberalisation in world trade that has fuelled radical alternatives to liberalism in the form of religious or ethnic fundamentalism. Of course, Huntington is right to argue that human rights cannot simply be imposed upon states suspicious of Western calls for democratic reform. However, Huntington's alternative to human rights, a rejection by Western states of multiculturalism domestically and an assertion of their identity internationally, is hardly likely to build common interests. There is a good chance that Huntington's approach, if adopted by states, would be a self-fulfilling prophecy and would only hasten the zero sum conflict between competing civilisations that he fears.

Huntington fails to see that it is the state that is the problem, not diverse cultures. This is illustrated by the fact that many of the conflicts in world politics since 1945 have been between states who Huntington says share the same culture; for example the Korean war or the two Gulf wars of the 1980s and 1990s. The reality is that conflict is inherent in the states system. This is built upon mutual suspicion between states, even where states may share a common culture or ethnic origin. Huntington also ignores how advocates of human rights have attempted to uphold universal rights, even in states which have very different cultures.

In 1999, for example, a US-led NATO intervened militarily to stop human rights abuses by Serbia against the people of Kosovo, who are predominately Muslim. Again, it is difficult to understand such actions within the logic of Huntington's clash of civilisations thesis. The central problem with Huntington's theory is that it is culturally deterministic. A world of multiple cultures is of course both inevitable and desirable, but if these differences are to be reconciled peacefully it is the nature of political and economic links through which states interact that are crucial. This is also true of relationships within the state between different cultural groups. Given Huntington's rejection of multicultural institutions as a way forward for liberal states, it is difficult to see how, for example, the 20 million or so Muslims who reside in Western states can be considered as equal citizens. In this regard, Huntington underestimates the culpability of liberal states in their hypocritical advocacy of human rights while at the same time promoting the further deregulation of world trade which undermines basic rights. The West has also given considerable support to authoritarian regimes, such as Saddam Hussein's Iraq during the 1980s. Such hypocrisy, and the subsequent inequalities that derive from such actions, will only drive already alienated minorities towards fundamentalist reactions against liberal values. In the words of Wallerstein (1995: 161), 'the self-contradiction of liberal ideology is total. If all humans have equal rights . . . we cannot maintain the kind of inegalitarian system that the capitalist world economy has always been and always will be.'

A third and more potentially fruitful alternative to Soysal's passive view of citizenship and Huntington's rejection of universal human rights theories does exist. I would argue that the roots of citizenship lie within individual communities, and rights and responsibilities will be expressed largely within this local context. However, globalisation demands that the roots of citizenship grow outwards to encompass obligations to other communities and the exercise of rights within a variety of contexts. As Lister (1997: 196) has argued, an inclusive notion of citizenship, which attempts to live up to liberal aspirations to equality of all persons, must necessarily be both internationalist and multi-layered. Citizenship is best thought of, suggests Lister, in terms of a 'spectrum that extends from the local through to the global'. This is what Heater has called multiple citizenship. A conception of multiple citizenship underscores the need to separate citizenship from limiting cultural identities such as nationality. The flexibility of mind required by a multi-textured view of citizenship also makes multiple citizenship incompatible with a citizenship based upon group identity such as advocated by Kymlicka and Young. As Heater (1990: 320) argues, 'it is necessary to accept as perfectly feasible the notion that an individual can have multiple civic identities and feel multiple loyalties'.

This third approach to citizenship is central to theories of cosmopolitan democracy advanced by such writers as David Held (1995). Cosmopolitan democracy seeks to theorise a citizenship that is global in its orientation and involves not just the protection of rights but also the extension of responsibilities beyond the state and the development of global institutions of governance. It is only by extending the responsibilities that diverse cultures have to respect each other's rights, together with the construction of more participatory institutions of global governance, that rights will be sustainable. This is because human governance is concerned with the problem of order and the distribution of material and cultural resources. As threats to social order increasingly occur at the level beyond the state, new political institutions are therefore required to meet these challenges. Similarly, globalisation has intensified levels of inequality across the globe and made the inequity in the distribution of resources more apparent. As Held (1995: viii) observes, the key challenge in political theory today is how institutions and concepts previously associated with the state can be adapted to the management of such global problems. Ways will need to be found to apply the constituent parts of citizenship, namely rights, responsibilities and participation, to both regional and global bodies of governance.

Rights remain crucial to any reconceptualised model of cosmopolitan democracy. Rights are the best mechanisms we have for signifying human dignity and autonomy. The problem, however, with the liberal tradition is that the rights it has defended have been highly abstract and disembodied. Given that in practice liberals have also embraced the state as the basic unit of politics, rights have been disconnected from an interdependent view of human relations and have tended to be enjoyed only by privileged individuals within privileged states. If we do not recognise the essentially relational nature of rights, and the way in which all rights depend upon recognition of others to be meaningful, then rights will have a limited impact on global problems.

However, processes of globalisation are beginning to change our perception of the nature of rights. First, as I have argued, the new security dilemmas associated with cross-border threats such as nuclear annihilation or ecological disaster are making states more sensitive to the rights of others. Injustices and rights violations within states can no longer be so easily contained, and state sovereignty is undoubtedly being challenged by the extension of arguments for human rights and by a more vigorous UN. The UN charter makes no mention of humanitarian intervention and yet the UN is increasingly intervening in the internal affairs of states to protect basic human rights. Although UN operations in Iraq, Rwanda, Somalia and Bosnia in the 1990s have had mixed results, the important principle of intervention on humanitarian grounds is being established. In 1994 the International War Crimes Tribunal was set up by the UN to investigate and prosecute perpetrators of crimes against humanity carried out in the war in Bosnia that followed the break-up of Yugoslavia. This body followed a precedent established after the Second World War at the Nuremberg trials, where Nazis responsible for appalling acts of genocide found that a defence based upon following the orders of one's government was not acceptable.

Regional bodies that are attempting to manage the problems associated with globalisation, such as the European Union (EU), are also extending citizenship rights beyond the boundaries of individual states. In fact the EU is unique amongst regional economic bodies because unlike, say, the North American Free Trade Agreement or Association of Southeast Asian Nations, it has looked to create political and not just economic institutions of cooperation. In the 1990s in particular the EU has made significant strides towards political union. At the centre of the project has been the creation of European Union citizenship, established formally through the Maastricht Treaty of 1992. This innovative development extended civil, and some political rights to all individuals who were members of EU countries. Citizens of member states can also vote to send representatives to the European Parliament, a body that has seen its powers of scrutiny and policy-making grow in the 1990s. Although the extension of citizenship in the EU has been problematic, as shall be discussed below, it has been significant in enhancing the autonomy and resources of women, part-time workers and working parents in particular (Meehan 1993).

The second way that globalisation is challenging an abstract view of rights is by enhancing awareness of threats to the eco-structure and therefore humanity's vulnerability to harm caused by ecological damage. This is why Turner's (1993) argument that an ontology for rights at the global level could be provided by the acceptance of human frailty is so useful. This idea captures the relational nature of citizenship in a way that the atomistic logic of liberals such Hobbes and Locke fails to grasp. A relational view of rights demands not only that we find ways to extend the benefits of rights to all peoples, regardless of national boundaries, it also means recognising that rights are only sustainable if we display a much greater sense of responsibility to other communities and to our natural environment. Global citizenship must involve responsibilities as well as rights. The rapid growth of ecological political thought in recent years has helped sensitise us to this issue in relation to the conservation of natural resources and a shift towards sustainable development which does not contribute to such phenomena as global warming or acid rain. An ecological dimension to citizenship involves extending the ethic of care, central to many feminist accounts of citizenship, which I discussed in chapter 5.

First, the ecological citizen is increasingly 'aware of his or her organic process of birth and growth out of the earth as a living organism' (Van Steenbergen 1994: 150). Such a conception of citizenship challenges the male-dominated, disembodied perspective on citizenship which has been central to liberalism and which has encouraged an atomistic approach to the question of rights and responsibilities. Second, ecological citizenship means extending our understanding of citizenship beyond material concerns with welfare rights and rights to property and market exchange (Steward 1991: 68). A consideration of ecological citizenship helps us to see the conceptual links between intimate citizenship and global problems. By taking care to be responsible in our own relationships, consumer patterns, and in the way we treat our environment generally, individuals can begin to make the shift away from purely quantitative measures of human success towards deeper and more qualitative assessments – such as the quality of the air we breathe, natural beauty and the enjoyment of freshly produced food (Steward 1991: 67). Understood in this way, citizenship makes an important challenge to the semiotic dominance of market-orientated language that has stressed narrow economic criteria as the primary measurement of human achievements. As Newby (1996: 210) has remarked, environmentalism has led to a much sharper recognition of the fact that 'economic wellbeing in itself does not promote civility, social cohesion or even a sense of enlightened self-interest'.

Third, the idea of limitless progress associated with liberalism, scientific innovation and economic growth is clearly being challenged by globalisation, which is revealing the limits of modernity. Ecological citizenship requires that we treat issues of conservation as at least as important as issues of 'progress' in science and economics. Thus the responsibilities we have as citizens extend not only to those with whom we currently share our community or planet, they also extend towards other species, the environment, and future generations of citizens. Smith (1998: 91) contends that citizenship needs to be underpinned by eco-centric as opposed to anthropocentric values. Even if we do not wish to accept that animals or natural forms have rights as such, we do need to acknowledge and exercise our responsibilities towards them.

Rethinking citizenship in response to worries about the environment is a good example of how global risks are demanding that we detach citizenship from its association with limiting concepts such as the nation-state or the public–private divide. As implied by the idea of intimate citizenship, ecological citizenship will also involve taking the notions of rights and responsibilities more seriously in non-conventional settings, such as in the family, in the supermarket (by the consumer choices we make) and in the context of the workplace. Ecological citizenship represents a deeper conception of citizenship than that offered by classical liberalism. Many of the responsibilities associated with this form of post-liberal citizenship will be voluntary obligations rather than enforceable duties. However, individual actions in terms of recycling, responsible consumer patterns and so on can only form part of the response to the challenges presented by globalisation. As well as establishing the framework of educational and political institutions through which this new citizenship can develop, governments must also display a greater willingness to exercise responsibilities beyond their boundaries. The current world order is structured firmly around the interests of states, and international law is still concerned with the activities of states rather than individuals. An important step towards a more global citizenship must therefore be a greater willingness for states to exercise global obligations and build stronger links with other countries.

Western states in particular must recognise the ways in which the world's political and economic systems are organised in ways that favour their interests over those of the rest of the globe. Appalling levels of poverty, debt and political instability in Africa, for example, are largely the legacy of the slave trade, colonialism and the unethical practices of Western companies. This is not, of course, to excuse political and economic elites generally from failing to honour their obligations to their own citizens as well as to the global community. To take the example of Africa again, dictators such as Mobuto Sese Seko, who ran a corrupt regime between 1965 and 1997 in the former Zaire, have contributed much to the suffering of Africans. However, it is Western states that possess the economic and political clout necessary to restructure the global order in ways that extend the responsibilities of citizenship to embrace obligations towards non-nationals.

There are many ways in which states can recognise their obligations. Western states could write off the debts that developing countries owe to them. As of 1999, for every £1 given by rich countries in the form of aid, poor countries return £4 in debt repayments (Jubilee 2000, 1999: 2). Many of these debts are the result of the legacy of imperialism and the low prices that the raw materials – the production of which many developing countries rely upon – fetch on the world markets. These prices themselves reflect the inequality of power between buyer and seller. Agriculture in the developing world is also jeopardised by such policies as the Common Agricultural Policy (CAP) in

Europe, which pays huge subsidies to farmers and thus creates unfair competition to Third World farmers. By writing off debt, aid to developing countries would become meaningful and could help to encourage sustainable development. By the end of 1999, there were some positive signs in this regard; President Clinton announced his intention to cut debts to zero providing more money was directed towards health and education programmes by Third World governments. Debt cancellation must also be accompanied by much more generous aid provision, which not only will help to stimulate economic activity in developing countries, but will also help to maintain political stability. A fairer and more tightly regulated trade regime is also necessary. This means ensuring that unjust policies, such as the EU's CAP, are rethought and monopolies that exist in industries like agriculture, which ensure the suppression of prices for raw materials, are broken up. A tax on money made through currency speculation would also help stabilise financial markets and therefore prices. This money could be used to fund global institutions of governance such as the UN.

As Dauenhauer (1996) has argued, rich states can also help development in poorer countries by avoiding adding to the 'brain drain' whereby skilled workers are poached by Western states. States must be more open and consistent in immigration policy and should shift towards criteria based upon the needs of immigrants rather than purely assessing applicants in terms of their financial viability. The record of liberal states here, however, is still poor in most cases. A good example of cynical immigration policies occurred when the British government, following the ending of Hong Kong's status as a British colony, chose to bestow citizenship only upon a few thousand of the most skilled and wealthy members of Hong Kong in the 1990 Nationality Act (O'Leary 1998). Instead of seeking only to import more expertise into wealthy countries through selective immigration policy, technologically advanced states should instead be more ready to share their innovations with others. This is one of the few areas of world trade that requires further liberalisation. Currently, the technology used by many MNCs is shrouded in secrecy and host states are prevented from sharing in such expertise, even though their citizens are employed by MNCs. Poorer countries cannot hope to compete in an increasingly technological and knowledge-driven market if they are denied access to inventions by strict copyright and patenting laws.

I have outlined briefly just a few examples of how states can exercise global citizenship by respecting the rights of other peoples, honouring existing responsibilities and looking to extend obligations that build trust between diverse communities. Unless rights and responsibilities of global citizenship are linked to the democratisation of decision-making bodies that govern world affairs, however, their existence will remain precarious. If we take human rights as an example, it is clear that the selective use of these doctrines does much to increase suspicions among non-Western states that human rights are little more than the assertion of Western interests by other means. Noam Chomsky (1997) gives many examples of how human rights have been used by the West as a propaganda tool against perceived opponents of liberalism while a blind eye has been turned to abuses in countries that are seen as important political or economic partners. Thus the USA, for instance, has been prepared to commit large resources in response to Iraq's invasion of Kuwait in 1990, but has failed to put sufficient pressure on Israel to abide by several UN declarations to withdraw from the West Bank and other territories that Israel holds illegally. As long as institutions of global governance such as the UN, the World Bank and the IMF are dominated by a small group of states, it is unlikely that the reciprocal trust that must underpin the rights and responsibilities of citizenship can extend to meet the challenges of globalisation identified in this chapter. Threats that conservatives like Huntington identify to world order, and particularly all forms of fundamentalism, are largely an understandable reaction by the non-Western world to the exclusionary practices, double standards and the hostility of Western policies in the international arena, rather than the result of fixed and conflicting cultures as Huntington suggests. Yet, democracy and human rights are powerful and emancipatory ideas, and authoritarian governments have found it hard to suppress popular demonstrations in favour of these principles in countries like East Timor, China and Iran. In each of these three examples, there have been mass demonstrations during the 1980s and 1990s in favour of democratic reform and the protection of basic rights. What this suggests is that a policy of constructive engagement by the West rather than the hostility implied by the clash of civilisations thesis is the most likely to extend the values of citizenship to the international level.

In seeking to build systems of global governance, however, it would be unwise to aim at the creation of a world state. As Arendt has remarked, 'the establishment of one sovereign world state . . . would be the end of all citizenship' (cit. in Baubock 1994: 15). Advocates of cosmopolitan democracy appear to recognise the problem that the states system raises for global governance and the security of rights. Held (1995: 268) writes,

> the Westphalian model, with its core commitment to the principle of effective power – that is, the principle that might eventually makes right in the international world – is at loggerheads with any requirement of sustained democratic negotiation among members of the international community.

Merely recreating the state form at a higher level of organisation would not tackle the problem that violence, concentrated primarily in the state, raises for democratic citizenship.

Crucially, multiple citizenship does not entail the destruction of separate political communities but rather seeks to transform the nature of the relationship between these communities. Held (1995: 267–86) uses the term 'overlapping networks of power' in contrast to the concentration of power in the state that has set the limits of citizenship in modernity. According to the principles of cosmopolitan citizenship, the individual will increasingly become used to exercising rights and responsibilities in a number of contexts and political communities. This suggests the need to transcend the concept of sovereignty, which a deep sense of citizenship must be opposed to, rather than seek to divide sovereignty as Held suggests we should (ibid.: 138). Hoffman has shown how Held's position is in fact inconsistent. As Hoffman (1998a: 62) notes, while Held's theory has an underlying post-statist logic, Held 'is unwilling to detach sovereignty from the state. He insists that the modern state is not defunct but rather that "its idea" must be adapted to "stretch across borders".' The danger of reforming, but retaining the concept of the state can be illustrated by the EU's attempt to construct political union through the extension of citizenship to the supranational level. The ambiguity of the EU project in general, and its associated form of citizenship in particular, symbolises the wider tensions that are increasingly shaping global politics.

As has been noted, the EU appears to represent a unique attempt in modernity to extend the rights of citizenship beyond the state. This, it seems to me, is a step in the right direction towards a multiple citizenship model suggested by cosmopolitan democracy. Through the growing powers of the European Parliament in particular, European citizenship is being linked to new forms of political participation that are encouraging closer cooperation between political parties, pressure groups and social movements across national boundaries. However, such positive developments must be balanced by an acknowledgement that for many policy makers in the EU, the citizenship project of the Union retains a distinctly statist and exclusive character. This can be demonstrated by the EU's approach to questions of third country nationals.

Unfortunately, the creation of EU citizenship at Maastricht failed to take an excellent opportunity to sever the link between nationality and citizenship. According to EU law, member states can still assert their right to determine citizenship of their communities and, in turn, EU citizenship is limited to those individuals who are legitimate citizens of member states. As O'Leary (1998: 91) insightfully comments, 'surely the whole point of Union citizenship was that it was a status which was to recognise an individual's rights (and duties) outside the traditional context of nation and state'.

It is this exclusive aspect of the EU that helps to highlight the weakness in the arguments of Soysal (1994: 148), who sees in the EU 'postnational membership in its most elaborate legal form' and that illustrates the contradictions inherent in the idea of divided sovereignty as advanced by Held. O'Leary (1998: 100) argues that far from being a postnational organisation, the EU is in fact attempting to encourage an exclusive (and mythical) European identity that sets cultural as well as legal limits on the expansion of citizenship. The Amsterdam Treaty of 1997 has further highlighted the negative implications of an EU superstate for asylum seekers and immigrants, by firming up common border controls. The Maastricht Treaty asserted the EU's support for human rights. However, at Amsterdam, it was agreed that the European Court of Justice would have no jurisdiction in the area of 'law and order and safeguarding of internal security' (Statewatch 1998: 13). Moreover, the 1997 treaty asserted that EU citizenship was to complement and not supersede national citizenship.

If the EU is to develop as an authentically democratic union that seeks to extend the freedoms associated with citizenship, it needs to address these contradictions by complementing the rights of EU citizenship with a Charter of Responsibilities that the EU has to poorer regions of the world and to the environment. This would need to include more extensive aid programmes, a reform of protectionism as found in the CAP, and a citizenship policy that breaks the link between nationality and citizenship and thereby creates a much greater liberalisation of immigration policy. As Bhabha (1998: 612) observes,

> Europe is creating a paradox while defining its territorial and social boundaries; failure to adhere to human rights norms excludes states from membership of the EU, but individuals excluded from access or membership frequently are denied those core constitutive protections in the process.

The future of citizenship turns upon the ways in which the problems raised by innovative but contradictory institutions of governance such as the EU are tackled. Falk (1995: 140) is surely right to state that in considering the future of citizenship, we cannot be overly constrained by what appears to be 'realistic' in the short term: 'global citizenship of a positive variety implies a utopian confidence in the human capacity to exceed realistic horizons, but it is also rooted in the highly pragmatic conviction that what is currently taken to be realistic is not sustainable'. Falk puts his finger on the challenges globalisation raises for citizenship. Advocates of global citizenship are not abstract utopians. They seek to build upon actual social changes that are making a modernist approach to citizenship untenable.

We should not give way to false optimism, however. Globalisation without doubt presents us with opportunities to extend the egalitarian thrust of liberal citizenship to its logical end, but globalisation also brings with it considerable dangers. In considering four possible scenarios for the future, ranging from an inclusive world citizenship, a disintegrative scenario of trade wars and ethnic violence, a globe dominated by a large political bloc involving the West and former Communist states, and the development of an exclusive Western regional fortress, Rapoport (1997: 113) considers the latter the most plausible. Privileged citizens of the West may well have rights that extend beyond their immediate locality, but these will come at the expense of the poor regions of the world. The essence of the argument presented in this chapter, and indeed throughout this book, has been that such a scenario could not hope to secure the rights of individuals and stable governance in the medium to long term given the rapid social changes that are transforming human relationships in late modernity.

Implicitly I have argued that a conception of citizenship in a global age must be postmodern in character. In terms of guaranteeing rights and ensuring the fulfilment of the responsibilities that any form of stable governance requires, it is no longer possible to retain the link between citizenship and the closed and exclusive form of political community that is the state, whether that state be national or regional in character.

7

CONCLUSION

The arguments advanced in this book suggest the need for what I have called a postmodern citizenship. In this final chapter, I first review the arguments that have led me to this conclusion. I then outline some features of a postmodern citizenship, before ending with a consideration of the future of the concept.

THE DEVELOPMENT OF CITIZENSHIP: A SUMMARY

Before the formation of modernity, citizenship was invariably an exclusive status. In some cases, particularly in the ancient Athenian polis, citizenship was undoubtedly deep, in the sense that citizens felt a strong commitment to common institutions of government and the obligations that citizens were expected to perform were extensive. Citizens themselves were entrusted to be rulers, as well as the ruled, and the polis's democratic and highly participatory system of governance reflected this. But in the pre-modern world the extent of citizenship was never broad in its scope, as it did not include large sections of the population.

Women especially were excluded from citizenship. In pre-modern society, the division between citizen and non-citizen signified inequalities that were taken to be natural and immutable.

The development of liberalism from the seventeenth century onwards marked a profound shift in the meaning of citizenship. Thinkers such as Hobbes and Locke introduced the notion of equality into debates concerning the relationship between the individual and state. For Locke and Paine, all individuals have indivisible rights to life, liberty and property. It is the main task of the political community to guarantee and protect these freedoms.

The conception of equality defended by liberals has, of course, been abstract in character. But by identifying the inherent equality of worth that all humans share, liberals did create the conceptual space for radicals to exploit. I understand socialism, for example, to be a post-liberal theory precisely because socialism challenges liberal society to make its promises of equality, security and justice *real for everyone*. A post-liberal approach to citizenship entails the identification of the political, economic and social barriers that prevent the rights and respon-sibilities of citizenship from being fairly distributed. Thus, socialists in the twentieth century have struggled to extend the franchise and to make markets more accountable to government. Post-liberals, then, take the context of citizenship more seriously than do liberals. They recognise that the structures of decision-making, economic production, and social institutions, such as the family, all play a significant part in determining the content, extent and depth of citizenship. The limits of citizenship in its liberal form can be explained, above all, by liberalism's neglect of this social context of rights and responsibilities. Why do liberals overlook the barriers to citizenship?

In chapter 3, I showed how a liberal defence of rights rests upon a set of assumptions that privileges the self-interest of the rational, egotistical individual over the needs of political community. Because liberals assume that we are autonomous actors, even before the formation of the state, arguments for liberal rights are abstract in form and miss, or underestimate, how rights, crucial though they are, must be rooted in a network of responsibilities between individuals and their communities. Like socialism, contemporary theories of republicanism and communitarianism are post-liberal because they stress the relational and non-hierarchical character of citizenship. Post-liberals, then, stress autonomy rather than liberty as a defining characteristic of citizenship. Autonomy is understood as *grounded independence*, rather than merely a licence to pursue one's interests without regard to the requirements of civic duty. A post-liberal approach to citizenship demands that rights and responsibilities be treated as mutually supportive, rather than opposed as many liberal theories have implied.

Our individual rights are only meaningful when they are supported by a sense of obligation amongst others both to recognise our rights and to help us to build and sustain the social institutions that make rights possible. This is why in chapters 3 and 5 I agreed with critics of liberal citizenship who insist that we must enhance our level of responsibility to our political communities. Postmodern societies are highly diverse and individualistic, and ways need to be found to create common interests and to develop social obligations (Beck 1997). There must be a degree of consensus over the values that underpin citizenship, if modern societies are not to fragment further and thereby become increasingly hard to govern effectively. The object of increasing duties, such as the responsibility to vote or to perform community service (both of which I have advocated), is to create the conditions whereby legal sanctions might gradually be transformed into a sense of voluntary obligation between diverse individuals. By enhancing responsibilities, we also acknowledge citizenship as an active and not a passive status.

Participation by all citizens, to the best of their ability, is essential if the content of citizenship is to be agreed democratically. By linking rights and responsibilities to an ethic of participation, citizenship can be reconceptualised as a *holistic* idea, as opposed to the *dualistic* conception of citizenship found in liberalism's defence of abstract rights.

Feminist and ecological critiques have highlighted how other aspects of liberalism's defence of abstract individualism have had negative implications for the practice of citizenship. Feminist accounts of citizenship have shown how liberal citizenship is a *disembodied* notion. In liberalism, citizenship has tended to be concerned with contractual relationships, market exchanges and the independence of the individual. Thus, the relationships between individuals are understood in atomistic terms. Feminists, in contrast, insist that the rights and responsibilities we have as citizens have to be linked to a recognition of the importance of the body. As Lister (1997: 70–2) argues, too often in traditional political theory the body, emotion and sexuality are seen as intrinsically female traits that hinder the application of reason, which must, liberals argue, lie at the heart of citizenship. Only once we realise that all individuals, regardless of their gender, have physical and emotional needs, are we likely to conceive of citizenship in terms of the values of interdependence and care. Moreover, these values, argue ecologists, must be extended beyond direct human need. In particular, humans must acknowledge their obligations to the environment, to other species, and to future generations. A postmodern approach to citizenship draws upon such post-liberal theories as socialism, feminism and ecologism.

A POSTMODERN CITIZENSHIP?

In modernity, the nature of citizenship has been determined by a paradox. A main theme of this book has been how the identification of citizenship with the nation-state has limited the universality and egalitarian ideals of liberalism. I demonstrated in chapter 2 how the French Revolution was the key event that fused the cultural idea of nationality with the political status of citizen. The pressures of war and revolutionary upheaval led to the abandonment of the more inclusive elements of the French Revolution, expressed in the defence of universal rights. Consequently, citizenship in the nineteenth and twentieth centuries has been closely associated with nation-building and military duty. Not only did the firming up of state boundaries mean a greater division between citizens and strangers, it also had major implications for the extent of citizenship *within* state boundaries. Writers such as Balibar (1994) and Yuval-Davis (1997) have shown how the nation-state is defined in gendered and racial terms. Women, for example, are portrayed as the 'mothers of the nation' who must be protected and kept 'pure' by their male defenders. The widespread use of rape as a military tool, particularly in ethnic wars of the 1980s and 1990s in such countries as Yugoslavia, is an example of how women are perceived as symbols and possessions of the nation, rather than as full citizens, equal to men. As well as being gendered, the state is also racialised. My analysis in chapter 2 of that most republican of states, contemporary France, shows how an apparent neutrality towards citizenship in fact masks a deep-seated racism and pathology towards immigrants.

The weaknesses of many traditional post-liberal and more contemporary postmodern theories are that they fail to identify the problem that the existence of the state creates for a universal citizenship. While reforms of the state, to enhance the democratic and inclusive nature of its institutions, are a necessary move, they are not a sufficient step towards fulfilling citizenship's potential. As long as we live in a world divided by territorial states, which are invariably defined in ethnic and gendered terms, citizenship's egalitarian logic will remain unfulfilled. I have argued, therefore, that a progressive postmodern citizenship must be detached from its modernist associations with the state.

It is important to remember that the main function of citizenship is to govern society according to the principles of respect for others' rights and an obligation to play a part in the maintenance of common institutions that sustain these rights. Violence, concentrated above all by the state, negates these principles of citizenship. As was suggested in chapter 5, a consideration of intimate citizenship, where rights and obligations create consensual rather than oppressive relationships within the private sphere, must also be extended to a consideration of the wider problem of state violence. A recognition of the problem violence creates for *all* human relationships means that a postmodern citizenship problematises both the state and the public–private divide. We cannot seek consensual relations in one sphere and rely upon force in the other. Postmodern citizenship is deep because it applies the values of rights and responsibilities to all human relationships, whether they be public or private in character.

In this context, Heater's (1990) notion of multiple citizenship seems to be the most appropriate form for citizenship, given both the plurality of modern society and the recent growth in the number and type of social and political institutions in which citizenship can be exercised. The flexibility of mind required to perform citizenship in a variety of contexts underlines the dangers of associating citizenship with only one narrow aspect of identity, such as nationality, ethnicity or group membership. In chapter 4, I argued against advocates of differentiated citizenship, where this means that we are asked to privilege one aspect of our identity over equally valued identities. The attractiveness of citizenship is that it does not force us to make a choice about what constitutes our essential nature. Instead it encourages us to conduct relationships with other citizens which are deliberative and open-ended. A citizenship based upon groups would most likely increase mutual suspicion and would endanger the rights of 'deviant individuals' within groups. Postmodern citizenship, I have suggested, must build upon and not reject liberals' defence of individual rights. Only through individual rights can real diversity, based upon individual choice and not pre-determined cultural identities, be maintained.

The best form of political community, then, for a postmodern citizenship is one where constitutional patriotism, rather than cultural ties, generates a sense of loyalty and obligation (Habermas 1994). This does mean that diverse cultures or even nationality disappear. For the foreseeable future, citizenship will still be exercised primarily at a local level. But what postmodern citizenship demands is that the boundaries between political communities are not perpetually closed, either materially or culturally, and that many of the rights and responsibilities of citizenship extend beyond administrative boundaries.

THE FUTURE OF CITIZENSHIP

Recent processes of social change, associated primarily with globalisation, appear to be creating the opportunity for the development of postmodern citizenship. Human rights, for example, are undoubtedly much more pervasive in their influence than ever before. In the twenty-first century, abuses of individuals' basic rights by their own states are becoming increasingly difficult to defend. The international community has begun to take human rights abuses more seriously, witnessed by a growing number of humanitarian interventions in places like Iraq and Kosovo. We are also witnessing the embryonic growth of institutions of global governance, such as the UN, as well as a greater role for regional bodies like the EU that have at least the potential to move beyond statist models of citizenship.

The key aspect of globalisation which makes a postmodern citizenship more likely in the future is the threat posed by planetary risks. According to liberals like Hobbes, the security and social order upon which any stable conception of citizenship must rest is best guaranteed by the state. Global risk challenges this relationship between citizenship and the state by undermining the state's capacity to provide security to its citizens. As theorists of cosmopolitan democracy assert, institutions of governance, as well as rights and responsibilities, must extend beyond the state if the very basis of human society is not to be destroyed by ecological disaster or by nuclear calamity (Held 1995).

Shaw (1994) argues that globalisation has helped to create what he calls a post-military society. I have noted how premodern and modern forms of citizenship have been associated closely with military duty. The coming of a post-military society challenges this. By post-militarism, Shaw is not claiming that we have seen the end of armed conflict. But in the shadow of nuclear annihilation, total wars in the style of the First or Second World Wars are much less likely. Moreover, the mass conscription armies of the twentieth century, which are linked historically to the creation of the welfare state and therefore the extension of citizenship, are no longer necessary. Professional, high-tech armies now conduct warfare. This suggests that the long established link between military duty, masculinity and citizenship is being weakened. Opportunities for more care-orientated approaches to citizenship are created as the connection between violence and citizenship is increasingly problematised.

Even more importantly, globalisation has highlighted the problem material inequalities pose for the practice of citizenship. Global inequalities constantly threaten the rights of those living in the developing world. Furthermore, the communications revolution and the development of planetary risk have spread both the dangers and the awareness of these dangers to the Western world. I have argued in this book that to make citizenship meaningful, and to give individuals a real opportunity to utilise their rights and exercise their responsibilities, we must recognise that citizenship is always *resource-dependent*. Within the context of liberal society, I have made the case for a new approach to social rights that seeks to strike a better balance between the imperatives of the market and the requirements of citizenship. The policy most likely to ensure that rights and responsibilities are not undermined by the inherent inequalities and exploitative tendencies of capitalism is a guaranteed citizens' income. I argued in chapter 6, however, that ways must also be found to improve the material conditions of poorer states. This is a matter of both justice and self-interest. In the context of globalisation, no community's citizenship can be assured if huge inequalities are allowed to continue. Migration, international crime, regional conflicts and environmental damage are all fuelled by inequalities, and the effects of these new security risks will be increasingly felt by both the developed and developing worlds. Institutions of global governance must therefore abandon the divisive neoliberal approach to economic management that currently informs such bodies as the World Bank and the IMF. Rich states must recognise that the world economic system is skewed in their favour and many of their achievements have come at the expense of Third World countries. States and regional bodies like the EU must therefore be more willing to honour their responsibilities to developing countries and to offer more extensive aid to help develop the democratic institutions across the globe that are essential to the practice of citizenship everywhere.

My approach to citizenship in this book has been postmodern because it does not seek to reject liberalism, but rather to make its promises real. I therefore reject those postmodern accounts that are critical of what I see as the strengths of liberalism, in particular: equality, individual rights, perfectionism and universal citizenship. Citizenship does have a future in an increasingly global and postmodern age because its constituent parts – rights, responsibilities and political participation – are essential to human governance. We must recognise, however, that it is only by breaking the links modernity has forged between citizenship and exclusive notions such as the state and the market that citizenship's emancipatory potential can be fulfilled.

BIBLIOGRAPHY

Arblaster, A. (1994) *Democracy* (2nd edn). Buckingham: Open University Press.

Aristotle (1992) *The Politics*. London: Penguin.

Bali, S. (1997) 'Migration and refugees', in B. White, R. Little and M. Smith (eds) *Issues in World Politics*. Basingstoke: Macmillan, pp. 200–21.

Balibar, E. (1991) 'Es gibt keinen Statt: Racism and politics in Europe today', *New Left Review* 186, pp. 5–19.

Balibar, E. (1994) *Masses, Classes, Ideas*. London: Routledge.

Barbalet, J. (1988) *Citizenship*. Milton Keynes: Open University Press.

Barber, B. (1984) *Strong Democracy: Participatory Politics for a New Age*. Berkeley, CA: University of California Press.

Baubock, R. (1994) *Transnational Citizenship*. Aldershot: Edward Elgar.

Beck, U. (1997) *The Reinvention of Politics*. Cambridge: Polity Press.

Bell, D. (1976) *The Cultural Contradictions of Capitalism*. London: Basic Books.

Bellamy, R. (1992) *Liberalism and Modern Society*. Cambridge: Polity Press.

Bendix, R. (1996) *Nation-Building and Citizenship* (revised edn). New Brunswick: Transaction Publishers.

Bernstein, J. (1991) 'Right, revolution and community: Marx's "On the Jewish Question"', in P. Osborne (ed.) *Socialism and the Limits of Liberalism*. London: Verso, pp. 91–120.

Bhabha, J. (1998) '"Get Back to where you once belonged": Identity, citizenship, and exclusion in Europe', *Human Rights Quarterly* 20, pp. 592–627.

Booth, K. (1995) 'Dare not to know: International relations theory versus the future' in K. Booth and S. Smith (eds) *International Relations Theory Today*. Cambridge: Polity Press, pp. 328–50.

Bretherton, C. (1996) 'Universal human rights: Bringing people into global politics?', in C. Bretherton and G. Ponton, *Global Politics*. Oxford: Blackwell, pp. 247–73.

Broadbent, E. (1997) *The Rise and Fall of Economic and Social Rights*. London: Canadian High Commission.

Brubaker, R. (1992) *Citizenship and Nationhood in France and Germany*. Cambridge: Cambridge University Press.

Bubeck, D. (1995) *A Feminist Approach to Citizenship*. Florence: European University Institute.

Bull, H. (1977) *The Anarchical Society*. London: Macmillan.

Burke, E. (1968) *Reflections on the Revolution in France*. London: Penguin.

Calhoun, G. (1997) *Nationalism*. Buckingham: Open University Press.

Chomsky, N. (1997) *World Orders, Old and New* (revised edn). London: Verso.

Clarke, P. (1994) (ed.) *Citizenship: A Reader*. London: Pluto Press.

Clarke, P. (1996) *Deep Citizenship*. London: Pluto Press.

Coole, D. (1993) *Women in Political Theory*. Hemel Hempstead: Harvester Wheatsheaf.

Cox, R. (1998) 'The consequences of welfare reforms: How conceptions of social rights are changing', *Journal of Social Policy* 27 (1), pp. 1–16.

Crozier, M. (1975) 'Western Europe', in M. Crozier, S. Huntington and J. Watanuki, *The Crisis of Democracy*. New York: New York University Press, pp. 11–57.

Dagger, R. (1997) *Civic Virtues*. Oxford: Oxford University Press.

Dahl, R. (1961) *Who Governs? Democracy and Power in an American City*. New Haven: Yale University Press.

Dalton, R. (1996) *Citizen Politics* (2nd edn). New Jersey: Chatham House.

Dauenhauer, B. (1996) *Citizenship in a Fragile World*. Maryland: Rowan and Littlefield.

Esping-Anderson, G. (1990) *The Three Worlds of Welfare Capitalism*. Cambridge: Polity Press.

Etzioni, A. (1995) *The Spirit of Community*. London: Fontana Press.

Etzioni, A. (1997) *The New Golden Rule*. London: Profile Books.

Falk, R. (1995) *On Human Governance*. Cambridge: Polity Press.

Faulks, K. (1998) *Citizenship in Modern Britain*. Edinburgh: Edinburgh University Press.

Faulks, K. (1999) *Political Sociology*. New York: New York University Press.

Favell, A. (1997) *Philosophies of Integration: Immigration and the Idea of Citizenship in France and Britain*. Basingstoke: Macmillan.

Fierlbeck, K. (1998) *Globalizing Democracy*. Manchester: Manchester University Press.

Forsyth, M. (1987) *Reason and Revolution: The Political Thought of Abbé Sieyès*. Leicester: Leicester University Press.

Frazer, N. and Gordon, L. (1994) 'Civil citizenship against social citizenship' in B. Van Steenbergen (ed.) *The Condition of Citizenship*. London: Sage, pp. 90–107.

Fukuyama, F. (1992) *The End of History and the Last Man*. London: Hamilton.

Giddens, A. (1984) *The Constitution of Society*. Cambridge: Polity Press.

Giddens, A. (1985) *The Nation-State and Violence*. Cambridge: Polity Press.

Giddens, A. (1994) *Beyond Left and Right*. Cambridge: Polity Press.

Giddens, A. (1998) *The Third Way*. Cambridge: Polity Press.

Green, T. H. (1986) *Lectures on the Principles of Political Obligation*. Cambridge: Cambridge University Press.

Habermas, J. (1974) *Theory and Practice*. London: Heinemann.

Habermas, J. (1994) 'Citizenship and national identity' in B. Van Steenbergen (ed.) *The Condition of Citizenship*. London: Sage, pp. 20–35.

Hall, C. (1994) 'Rethinking imperial histories: The Reform Act of 1867', *New Left Review* 208, pp. 3–29.

Hayek, F. (1944) *The Road to Serfdom*. London: Routledge.

Heater, D. (1990) *Citizenship*. London: Longman.

Held, D. (1995) *Democracy and the Global Order*. Cambridge: Polity Press.

Held, D. (1996) *Models of Democracy* (2nd edn). Cambridge: Polity Press.

Himmelfarb, G. (1995) *The De-Moralization of Society*. London: IEA Health and Welfare Unit.

Hirst, P. (1994) *Associative Democracy*. Cambridge: Polity Press.

Hirst, P. and Thompson, G. (1996) *Globalization in Question*. Cambridge: Polity Press.

Hobbes, T. (1973) *Leviathan*. London: Dent.

Hoffman, J. (1995) *Beyond the State*. Cambridge: Polity Press.

Hoffman, J. (1997) 'Citizenship and the state'. Paper presented at the conference Citizenship for the Twenty-first Century at the University of Central Lancashire, October.

Hoffman, J. (1998) 'Is there a case for a feminist critique of the state?', *Contemporary Politics* 4 (2), pp. 161–76.

Hoffman J. (1998a) *Sovereignty*. Buckingham: Open University Press.

Horsman, M. and Marshall, A. (1995) *After the Nation-State*. London: HarperCollins.

Hunt, L. (1992) 'Afterword', in R. Waldinger, P. Dawson and I. Woloch (eds) *The French Revolution and the Meaning of Citizenship*. London: Greenwood Press, pp. 211–13.

Huntington, S. (1998) *The Clash of Civilisations and the Remaking of the World Order*. London: Touchstone.

Ignatieff, M. (1991) 'Citizenship and moral narcissism', in G. Andrews (ed.) *Citizenship*. London: Lawrence and Wishart, pp. 26–36.

Ivory, M. (1998) 'The Fife users' panel', *Community Care* 16–22 April, p. 13.

Johnston, P., Steele, J. and Jones, G. (1999) 'We must change as a nation', *Electronic Telegraph*, 25 February (www.telegraph.co.uk).

Joppke, C. (1998) 'Immigration challenges the nation-state' in C. Joppke (ed.) *Challenges to the Nation-State: Immigration in Western Europe and the United States*. Oxford: Oxford University Press, pp. 5–46.

Jordan, B. (1989) *The Common Good*. Oxford: Blackwell.

Jubilee 2000 (1999) *The Jubilee 2000 Campaign*. Jubilee2000.future.easy-space.ac.uk, pp.1–6.

Korten, D. (1995) *When Corporations Rule the World*. Connecticut: Kumarian.

Kostakopoulou, D. (1998) 'Is there an alternative to "Schengenland"?', *Political Studies* XLVI, pp. 886–902.

Kymlicka, W. (1990) *Liberalism, Community, and Culture*. Oxford: Oxford University Press.

Kymlicka, W. (1995) *Multicultural Citizenship*. Oxford: Oxford University Press.

Lister, R. (1997) *Citizenship: Feminist Perspectives*. Basingstoke: Macmillan.

Locke, J. (1924) *Two Treatises of Government*. London: Dent.

Lowe, R. (1993) *The Welfare State in Britain Since 1945*. London: Macmillan.

Malik, K. (1996) *The Meaning of Race*. Basingstoke: Macmillan.

Mann, M. (1993) *The Sources of Social Power*, vol. 2. Cambridge: Cambridge University Press.

Mann, M. (1996) 'Ruling class strategies and citizenship', in M. Bulmer and A. Rees (eds) *Citizenship Today*. London: UCL, pp. 125–44.

Manville, P. (1994) 'Towards a new paradigm of Athenian citizenship', in

A. Boegehold and A. Scafuro (eds) *Athenian Identity and Civic Ideology*. Baltimore, MD: Johns Hopkins University Press, pp. 21–33.

Marshall, T. H. (1981) *The Right to Welfare and Other Essays*. London: Heinemann.

Marshall, T. H. (1992) 'Citizenship and social class', in T. H. Marshall and T. Bottomore, *Citizenship and Social Class*. London: Pluto Press, pp. 1–51.

Marx, K. (1994) 'On the Jewish Question', in K. Marx, *Early Political Writings*. Cambridge: Cambridge University Press, pp. 28–56.

Marx, K. and Engels, F. (1962) *Selected Works*, vol. 1. Moscow: Foreign Languages Publishing House.

McLennan, G. (1995) *Pluralism*. Buckingham: Open University Press.

Mead, L. (1986) *Beyond Entitlement*. New York: Free Press.

Meehan, E. (1993) *Citizenship and the European Community*. London: Sage.

Migration News (1998) 'Germany: Dual citizenship, asylum, enforcement', *Migration News* 5 (1), pp. 1–2.

Mill, J. S. (1974) *On Liberty*. London: Penguin.

Miller, D. (1995) *On Nationality*. Oxford: Oxford University Press.

Miller, D. (1995a) 'Citizenship and pluralism', *Political Studies* XLIII, pp. 432–50.

Newby, H. (1996) 'Citizenship in a green world: Global commons and human stewardship', in M. Bulmer and A. Rees (eds) *Citizenship Today*. London: UCL Press, pp. 209–22.

Nicolet, C. (1980) *The World of the Citizen in Republican Rome*. London: Batsford.

Nozick, R. (1974) *Anarchy, State and Utopia*. Oxford: Blackwell.

O'Connor, J. (1998) 'US social welfare policy: The Reagan record and legacy', *Journal of Social Policy* 27 (1), pp. 37–61.

Ohmae, K. (1995) *The End of the Nation-State*. New York: Free Press.

Oldfield, A. (1990) *Citizenship and Community*. London: Routledge.

O'Leary, S. (1998) 'The options for the reform of European Union citizenship', in S. O'Leary and T. Tiilikainen (eds) *Citizenship and Nationality Status in the New Europe*. London: IPPR, pp. 81–116.

Oommen, T. (1997) *Citizenship, Nationality and Ethnicity*. Cambridge: Polity Press.

Paine, T. (1995) *Rights of Man, Common Sense and Other Political Writings*. Oxford: Oxford University Press.

Parker, H. (ed.) (1993) *Citizen's Income and Women*. London: Citizen's Income Study Centre.

Parker, J. (1998) *Citizenship, Work, and Welfare*. Basingstoke: Macmillan.

Pateman, C. (1988) *The Sexual Contract*. Cambridge: Polity Press.

Pateman, C. (1992) 'Equality, difference, subordination: The politics of motherhood and women's citizenship', in G. Bock and S. James (eds) *Beyond Equality and Difference*. London: Routledge, pp. 17–31.

Pettit, P. (1997) *Republicanism*. Oxford: Oxford University Press.

Phillips, A. (1993) *Democracy and Difference*. Cambridge: Polity Press.

Pierson, C. (1998) 'Contemporary challenges to welfare state development', *Political Studies* XLVI, pp. 777–94.

Pixley, P. (1993) *Citizenship and Employment*. Cambridge: Cambridge University Press.

Plant, R. (1992) 'Citizenship, rights and welfare', in A. Coote (ed.) *The Welfare of Citizens*. London: IPPR, pp. 15–29.

Plummer, K. (1999) 'Inventing intimate citizenship.' Paper presented at the conference Rethinking Citizenship, University of Leeds, June.

Rapoport, A. (1997) 'The dual role of the nation state in the evolution of world citizenship', in J. Rotblat (ed.) *World Citizenship*. Basingstoke: Macmillan, pp. 91–125.

Rees, A. (1995) 'The other T. H. Marshall', *Journal of Social Policy* 24 (3), pp. 341–62.

Riesenberg, P. (1992) *Citizenship in the Western Tradition*. Chapel Hill, NC: University of North Carolina Press.

Rousseau, J. J. (1968) *The Social Contract*. London: Penguin.

Schuck, P. (1998) 'The re-evaluation of American citizenship', in C. Joppke (ed.) *Challenges to the Nation-State: Immigration in Western Europe and the United States*. Oxford: Oxford University Press, pp. 191–230.

Schwarzmantel, J. (1998) *The Age of Ideology*. Basingstoke: Macmillan.

Selbourne, D. (1994) *The Principle of Duty*. London: Sinclair-Stevenson.

Shaw, M. (1994) *Global Society and International Relations*. Cambridge: Polity Press.

Shklar, J. (1991) *American Citizenship: The Quest for Inclusion*. Harvard: Harvard University Press.

Silverman, M. (1992) *Deconstructing the Nation: Immigration, Racism and Citizenship in Modern France*. London: Routledge.

Skinner, Q. (1978) *The Foundations of Modern Political Thought*, vol. 1. Cambridge: Cambridge University Press.

Skinner, Q. (1978a) *The Foundations of Modern Political Thought*, vol. 2. Cambridge: Cambridge University Press.

Smith, A. (1995) *Nations and Nationalism in a Global Era*. Cambridge: Polity Press.

Smith, M. (1998) *Ecologism*. Buckingham: Open University Press.

Soysal, Y. (1994) *Limits of Citizenship*. Chicago, IL: University of Chicago Press.

Statewatch (1998) 'Schengen and EU agree to extend fortress Europe', *Statewatch* 8 (1), pp. 1–3

Steward, F. (1991) 'Citizens of Planet Earth', in G. Andrews (ed.) *Citizenship*. London: Lawrence and Wishart, pp. 65–75.

Tam, H. (1998) *Communitarianism*. London: Macmillan.

Thomas, P. (1984) 'Alien politics: A Marxian perspective on citizenship and democracy' in T. Ball and J. Farr (eds) *After Marx*. Cambridge: Cambridge University Press, pp. 124–40.

Tilly, C. (1995) 'The emergence of citizenship in France and elsewhere', *International Review of Social History* 40 supplement 3, pp. 223–36.

Turner, B. (1986) *Citizenship and Capitalism*. London: Allen and Unwin.

Turner, B. (1993) 'Outline of a theory of human rights' in B. Turner (ed.) *Citizenship and Social Theory*. London: Sage, pp. 162–90.

Turner, B. (1994) 'Postmodern culture/modern citizens', in B. Van Steenbergen (ed.) *The Condition of Citizenship*. London: Sage, pp. 153–68.

Twine, F. (1994) *Social Rights and Citizenship*. London: Sage.

Van Parijs, P. (1995) *Real Freedom For All*. Oxford: Oxford University Press.

Van Steenbergen, B. (1994) 'Towards a global ecological citizen', in B. Van Steenbergen (ed.) *The Condition of Citizenship*. London: Sage, pp. 141–52.

Walby, S. (1990) *Theorising Patriarchy*. Oxford: Basil Blackwell.

Waldron, J. (1987) (ed.) *Nonsense Upon Stilts*. London: Methuen.

Waldron, J. (1992) 'Minority cultures and the cosmopolitan alternative', *University of Michigan Journal of Law Reform* 25 (3–4), pp. 751–93.

Wallerstein, I. (1995) *After Liberalism*. New York: New Press.

Waters, M. (1995) *Globalization*. London: Routledge.

Weber, M. (1958) *The City*. New York: Free Press.

Weeks, J. (1998) 'The sexual citizen', *Theory, Culture and Society* 15 (3–4) pp. 35–52.

Weiler, G. (1997) 'Logos against Leviathan: The Hobbesian origins of modern antipolitics', in A. Schedler (ed.) *The End of Politics?* Basingstoke: Macmillan, pp. 40–56.

Williams, R. (1997) *Hegel's Ethics of Recognition*. California: University of California Press.

Young, I. (1989) 'Polity and group difference: A critique of the ideal of universal citizenship', *Ethics* 99, pp. 250–74.

Young, I. (1990) *Justice and the Politics of Difference*. Princeton, NJ: Princeton University Press.

Yuval-Davis, A. (1997) *Gender and Nation*. London: Sage.

Index

Printed in Great Britain
by Amazon.co.uk, Ltd.,
Marston Gate.